Figure 1. Court portrait of a prince in a Western setting, mid-eighteenth century. The model could be Yongzhan, a brother of the Qianlong emperor. Painting on paper, courtesy Freer Gallery of Art/Arthur M. Sackler Gallery, Washington, D.C.

Barbarian Lens

Documenting the Image

A series edited by
Helene E. Roberts, *Visual Resources, Dartmouth College, Hanover, New Hampshire,* and Christine L. Sundt, *Visual Resources, University of Oregon, Eugene*

Documenting the Image describes the history, influences, and implications of visual artifacts. Its goals include publishing monographs and reference books that promote visual collections around the world.

Volume 1
An Introduction to Iconography: Symbols, Allusions and Meaning in the Visual Arts
Roelof van Straten
Translated by Patricia de Man

Volume 2
Art History through the Camera's Lens
Edited by Helene E. Roberts

Volume 3
"Remove Not the Ancient Landmark": Public Monuments and Moral Values
Edited by Donald M. Reynolds

Volume 4
"A Higher Branch of the Art": Photographing the Fine Arts in England, 1839–1880
Anthony J. Hamber

Volume 5
Landmarks of Russian Architecture: A Photographic Survey
William Craft Brumfield

Volume 6
Barbarian Lens: Western Photographers of the Qianlong Emperor's European Palaces
Régine Thiriez

Additional titles forthcoming

This book is part of a series. The publisher will accept continuation orders which may be cancelled at any time and which provide for automatic billing and shipping of each title in the series upon publication. Please write for details.

Barbarian Lens

Western Photographers of the Qianlong Emperor's European Palaces

Régine Thiriez

Routledge
Taylor & Francis Group
LONDON AND NEW YORK

First published 2017 by Routledge

2 Park Square, Milton Park, Abingdon, Oxfordshire OX14 4RN
52 Vanderbilt Avenue, New York, NY 10017

Routledge is an imprint of the Taylor & Francis Group, an informa business

First issued in paperback 2019

British Library Cataloguing in Publication Data

Thiriez, Régine
Barbarian lens : Western photographers of the Qianlong Emperor's European palaces. - (Documenting the image ; v.
6 - ISSN 1068–6894)
1. Yuan Ming Yuan (Peking, China) - History 2. Yuan Ming Yuan (Peking, China) - Pictorial works
I. Title
728.8'2'0951156

ISBN13: 978-90-5700-519-0 (hbk)
ISBN13: 978-1-138-00223-4 (pbk)

IN MEMORIAM

Hedda Morrison (1908–1991)

The death of Hedda Morrison on December 3, 1991, just ten days short of her eighty-third birthday, removes one of the last links with the small but astonishingly varied Western community that lived in Beijing in the 1930s. (A. Morrison, 1992).

Hedda Morrison, still known as Hedda Hammer, was a promising young photographer when she moved to Beijing in 1933 from Germany. She had been hired to manage the Hartung Photo Shop in Legation Street, which also created thematic albums of photographs of Beijing. Times were changing and, although a woman, she was in charge of a sizable staff of Chinese male workers. At the end of her contract in 1938, she turned to free-lance work.

In the late 1930s and early 1940s, during her free time she was taking personal "fotos" (sic) of everything in any way interesting to her (H. Morrison to author, April 15, 1990). This is how she made two small series of views of the European Palaces, which illustrate in the most striking way the final disasters that befell the site after 1925.[1] When Morrison made those images, Beijing was occupied by the Japanese army, and times were very hard; survival, not building conservation, was the priority. As a German national and therefore allied with Japan, the photographer was not deported like other Westerners; to the end of the war she retained her freedom to go around city and country with her bicycle, camera and what little film she could procure.

After the war she married Alastair Morrison, an Australian she had known in Beijing in 1940. Between 1947 and 1967, they lived in Sarawak (Malaysia); there, as she had done in China, she recorded places, customs, crafts and changing cultures. The couple moved to Canberra, Australia, in 1967. In addition to publications on Sarawak, two volumes of her Chinese photographs were published in recent years. She also contributed to the illustration of a number of books and articles.

Hedda Morrison is no longer in Beijing. The Beijing she knew does not survive either, except in photographs.

[1] Hedda Morrison's negatives were given to Harvard-Yenching library by Alastair Morrison. Views of the European Palaces are numbered S 8394 to 8407.

IN MEMORIAM

CONTENTS

Appendices

FIGURES

Photo Credits Numbers refer to figure numbers

Antoine Durand, Strasbourg, France: **15, 31, 32**
Author's Collection: **3, 4, 5, 8, 11, 12, 17, 20, 22, 24, 26, 27, 30, 33, 34, 36, 37, 38, 44, 48**
Bibliothèque Asiatique du Collège de France, Paris, France: **14**
Bibliothèque Nationale de France, Paris, France: **7, 21, 23**
Bibliothèque Thiers, Paris, France: **46**
Charles Blackburn, Neuilly, France: **13, 49, 50, 51**
Durham University Oriental Museum, Durham, UK: **18**
Ecole Nationale Supérieure des Beaux-Arts, Paris, France: **2**
Freer Gallery of Art/Arthur M. Sackler Gallery, Washington, DC, USA: **1, 54**
The Sidney D. Gamble Foundation for Chinese Studies, New York, USA: **40**
Hedda Morrison, Canberra, Australia: **41**
Musée d'Orsay, Paris: **6**
National Museum of Denmark, Dept. of Ethnology, Copenhagen, Denmark: **19, 28, 39, 55**
Peabody Essex Museum, Salem, Mass., USA: **9, 10, 25, 42, 45, 52**
Rare Book and Special Collections Library, University of Illinois at Urbana–Champaign, USA, reproduced by permission: **29**
Rockefeller Archive Center, North Tarrytown, NY, USA: **53, 56**
Royal Ontario Museum, Far Eastern Dept., Toronto, Canada: **43**
Stadtmuseum, Uslar, Germany: **16, 35, 46**

INTRODUCTION TO THE SERIES

Documenting the Image is devoted to describing the history, process, and use of visual documents. As many events and most artifacts are known and studied through images made of them, the study of the creation, collection, and use of these images becomes crucial to our understanding of the originals. *Documenting the Image* will provide an arena for discussion of the influence of visual documentation on culture, academic disciplines, and ways of thinking. It will inquire into how visual language is structured and how visual meaning is communicated. It will explore the visual documentation of artifacts through drawings, casts, facsimiles, engravings, and photography, and it will describe the effects of the new electronic technology on visual resources. Through the publication of catalogs of visual materials, it will seek to make these collections better known and more accessible to a wide range of potential users. In addition, the series will provide reference tools which support the description, organization, and use of visual collections.

PREFACE

Most works are born of interest for a subject; others from the availability of material. This one derives from sheer obstinacy in tracking elusive images, and from the ultimate realization that these same images were the gates to a wide and exciting world.

It all began in 1987 with a search for photographic documents. The subject was the European Palaces of the Yuanmingyuan, a Western-style architectural group built in the mid-eighteenth century near Beijing by Jesuit missionaries working for the Emperor of China. Torched during the 1860 Rape of the Summer Palace, the buildings have now almost entirely vanished. A group of French researchers had undertaken a study of the palaces and the garden they were built into, and I joined them to look for photographs to supplement the documentation.

My field up to that point had been the history of Chinese art or, more specifically, archeology. I also had a background in the general history of art, in which there had been no place for either nineteenth-century China or photography, and a masters degree in economy. If nothing else, this had taught me the value of statistics.

Surprisingly good, considering the odds, the results of the 1987 research were still much less—and much slower—than had been hoped for. Within a few weeks, it became clear that finding images of an architectural complex little known outside very specialized circles was a real challenge. I could soon define my task as "tracing hypothetical documents kept by unknown people who don't know anything about them." In the end, my investigations had covered a wide array of diverse fields: from collections of photography to ethnographic museums; from Chinese export art to porcelain, architecture and archeology; from the formation of major collections of Chinese artifacts in the United States to German diplomacy in East Asia at the turn of the century. I had sent hundreds of letters to people all over the world and received many answers. And I even found a few dozen photographs that were quite useful for the team's research.

I learned how to recognize albumen prints; to look for signs identifying the type of negative; to appreciate the quality of an original print, as opposed to a copy-print; to see how photographs were pasted onto album leaves (some Germans do only the corners); or how the glass plate of an autochrome differs from that of a silver gelatin negative.

Beyond the ruined walls and broken ceramics of a site I had come to know very well, I found people of a bygone age, and with them the China of old and its "barbarian" visitors.

My progress over the years was empirical. Each step was different from the one before. Each new field branched into several directions, some of them remarkably unexplored: As of today, whole relevant areas—the most important of which is probably early photography in China—are still to be documented.

I used some ready-made information; discovered much by trial, error and chance; and put it all together. The result was a picture of the times and the men who photographed the European Palaces. Names popped up—one of them turned out to be a great-great uncle, consul at Fuzhou in Fujian, of whom I had never heard—while gradually the image of post-1860 photography in China and Beijing became clearer. Beijing is a very good base for research on the beginnings of photography. It was practiced there in a quite distinctive way and, because the city was opened to foreigners only in 1860, there is a clear starting date. I was able to identify a number of early photographs and put names on some of them. Quite to my surprise, this added a leaf to the history of French photography. I looked into what made nineteenth-century Beijing photography specialize in monuments. The key, I believe, was Thomas Child, an Englishman who became my reference for that period. He photographed the Yuanmingyuan in 1877–78.

The two rules I defined on deciding to make a doctoral dissertation out of this material were first, I would always follow the material, as opposed to selecting it to make it fit a preconceived research model; and second, I would use primary sources whenever possible in order to stay close to the time period studied. Taking into account the vast quantity of unpublished original material, I also decided not to research subjects that had already been, or were being, treated elsewhere—even though my approach might have been different—unless I had already completed my own research. After collecting information from Hedda Morrison for several years, I discovered she was the object of studies in progress in Australia, and reluctantly abandoned my plans. What will be done by people who knew her much better than I ever could makes any study of mine redundant.

While some of the information I present here is relevant only to the European Palaces, I believe that most of it has a broader reach and could be used in other contexts. As a kind advisor once told me, to encourage me to expand on the subject—not that I needed encouragement, really—"After all, these [the palaces as photographed] are only ruins." All too true, alas. But the information I came across in the course of my research—whether on photographic processes, Beijing, the Customs services, or mercenaries fighting under the Chinese banner—was part of the picture and is presented here. I consider this book as an opening door to a variety of subjects. What it is *not*, is a final study on any given topic . . . including, I am quite certain, the photography of the European Palaces of the Yuanmingyuan.

During my years of research, I learned a great deal about missionary and foreign military operations in China, to no avail regarding the palaces. I also became knowledgeable about Imperial Chinese Maritime Customs and the development of the Postal Service, which proved more rewarding. I met with incredibly generous assistance and came in contact with deeply interested curators and librarians; I discovered much about their duties and how helpful they generally can be. I pondered the approach to consulting in different countries: open stacks or bulletins, photography allowed or purchase of prints required—my vote goes to the first in each case!

I followed many leads and developed a certain philosophy about them: Never believe something you do not check yourself. I made friends from the United States to Australia, spending time in libraries and archives in London, Edinburgh, Belfast—where I was awakened by a bomb blast on my birthday—and also in Hildesheim, Uslar and Hamburg in Germany. I looked into basements and back shelves in Toronto, Boston, Rochester, New York and Washington DC, and some other out-of-the-way exotic places. Any inventory of resources was very time consuming: I first had to determine from a distance if a trip would really be useful and how long it should be—on that, I was often wrong—and then either be able to stay long enough to finish or come back. Incredibly, I almost never stayed in hotels. Research would not go very far without hospitality and the patient ears that often go with it.

I wrote a few articles as I progressed. My method shifted wildly according to what I was finding and, even more so, how I was finding it. In the end, I gave up entirely on trying to build a framework suitable for each one of the people or photographs studied, and took what I found as I found it.

I became immersed in the period as it was, with its good and bad sides and its colossal political incorrectness. I started seeing things as they had been seen . . . with a difference. People who lived through that time cannot have experienced the awe I now feel for old photographs, for late Imperial China, for all the people who went to China for good or not-so-good reasons, for the Chinese who suffered their presence and, in general, for a world now gone forever but still close enough to be part of living memories.

My hitherto unknown great-great uncle met Thomas Child, Ernst Ohlmer and Théophile Piry, three photographers of the Yuanmingyuan. I discovered a single short reference to him in Piry's papers: "Poor Plichon has died" (in 1880 in Hong Kong). As a matter of fact, all the actors in this study have died. Perhaps they will live a little in our memories as a result of this book.

ACKNOWLEDGMENTS

In the course of nearly ten years of research, many debts were incurred. Numerous people were met during the search for photographs or documentation; they were a tremendous stimulus.

Most notable is Michèle Pirazzoli-t'Serstevens, who introduced me to Chinese art and civilization in 1974, received me in her seminar for many years afterwards, and invited me to join her research team on the European Palaces. There, my interest in photography and nineteenth-century China originated. As my thesis director, she saw the project through to its end, and deserves all the credit due her.

Heartfelt thanks go to those who believed in this research from the first day. It is no exaggeration to say that without them, this book would not have happened. Most special is Craig Clunas, who never spared his encouragement and scholarly advice, and proved the best of friends in repeatedly dealing with a very nervous author and a doctoral manuscript at diverse stages of "uncompletion." Likewise, over the years, Jeannie Parker has generously shared her in-depth knowledge of the Royal Ontario Museum East Asian collections, her hospitality, and sense of fun. She exercised superb editing skills on several earlier articles as well as on this manuscript.

Among the scholars who took an interest in the project were Marianne Bastid-Bruguière and Françoise Heilbrun, who were kind enough to sit on my jury. I also received valuable support from John K. Fairbank, George N. Kates and Philippe Neagu, all outstanding scholars whose passing is a measure of the time elapsed.

Fellow researchers on the European Palaces team, particularly Gilles and Marie-Pierre Genest, Antoine Durand and Vincent Droguet, provided perspective on the photographs and information on the European Palaces through their own research.

Special mention must go to Andreas Mixius for explaining things German, chauffeuring, translating, and generally being there, and to his wife Maria for assistance beyond the call of duty; to Sue Naquin for her unfailing support, drive, and provocative thought; to John Ward, for having the Science Museum in London generously print a rare set of negative glass plates that are the earliest photographs of the European Palaces; to Anne Chayet for the lengthy discussions when there was still time in our lives, and the little notes in the mail when there was none left. Generous Chinese-language assistance came from John Finlay and Cary Liu.

Hospitality contributed a large share in this research. Whether in the United States, Canada, Britain or Germany, Marge and Skip Motes, Jeannie Parker, Susan and Hermann Jenny, Lane O'Connor, John and Molly Glenn, Anne Muir, Roselyn Romberg and Douglas Hardy, Hélène and Edouard Thiriez—thank you again for your many kindnesses and unfailing patience with the vagaries of a single-minded researcher. Also, most specially, thank you to the memory of Sybil Rocci of Salem, Massachusetts, and to her daughters Sandy and Patti and their husbands Alex and Bruce.

Special thanks are due to the people who shared with me their family papers and withstood my repeated incursions with the greatest and most generous hospitality. First among these are Charles and Nina Blackburn, but also the Earl and Countess of Elgin, Catherine Curran and Frances Anner.

Many fellow researchers have been more than generous in their assistance. I would name most particularly Françoise Aubin, Katherine F. Bruner, Dennis G. Crow, Ulrich Hausmann, Gert Naundorf, Colin Osman, Nick Pearce, Dianne Reilly, John W. Witek, and Hartmut Walravens.

A great number of archivists, librarians and curators went out of their way to make my life easier and my research more effective, either directly or by mail, phone, fax or any means at their disposal. First would come Colleen Hennessey, Raymond Lum, Annie Salavert-Sablayrole, and Joan Hornby. And I must not forget Dr. Biewer, Dorie Dohrenwend, Jean Foiret, Douglas M. Haller, Peter Hardie, Elaine Hart, Jack Howard, Dr. Knödel, John Lundquist, I. H. McCausland, Margaretha Peijfors, J. H. Peters, Anne Pollen, Helene E. Roberts, Dr. Schäfer, Mette Siggstedt, William Stapp, Helga Stein, Lindsay Steward, Jan Stuart, Roberta Waddell, Beverly Williams, W. G. Wheeler, and Jean-Paul Wiest.

This project was supported by two research grants. A total of six months were spent in Salem, Massachusetts as a guest, alternatively, of the Peabody Museum and the Essex Institute, now joined into the Peabody Essex Museum. Françoise and Peter Fetchko's hospitality paved the way to a fuller use of the libraries and collections. Will La Moy, as head librarian and responsible for the fellowship committee, will find here a mark of my appreciation. Also tremendously helpful through the years, as well as real friends, were Kathy Flynn, John Koza, Beth and John Grimes, Crosby Forbes, and in general the whole staff of both institutions. Mark Sexton contributed his talent, time and considerable knowledge of photographic technique to this project.

The Rockefeller Archive Center provided a grant to research Conrad Anner. Darwin H. Stappleton and his staff, especially Thomas Rosenbaum and Emily J. Oakhill, who managed to make herself constantly available, helped make time flow very efficiently and pleasantly.

Last, a very fond thank you to the memory of a kind lady and wonderful photographer of the China of old, the late Hedda Morrison of Canberra, Australia, and deepest thanks to her husband Alastair Morrison.

INTRODUCTION

"European Palaces of the Yuanmingyuan, Beijing, 1747–1860," reads an imaginary memorial stone. For, to this day, the legendary Summer Palace, looted and put to the torch during the last of the "opium wars" in 1860, remains in memories. Nevertheless, beyond the extraordinary context of their construction by Jesuit missionaries—voluntary exiles at the court of one of the most powerful emperors of China—and their wanton destruction by other Westerners a mere century later, they are symbols to which few remain immune. Their evocative power is what makes the palaces a fascinating object of study.

However, the least-considered aspect of the European Palaces' history has been what happened after they had been "destroyed." It is generally known that since 1860 China has changed beyond recognition. But what of the palaces, their walls, the stones and ceramic tiles, their fountains and ornamental flowers? How did they become the polished and vacant enclosure shown to modern visitors as a symbol of China's suffering at foreign hands?

To these questions and many more, photography brought answers. But a photograph without an author and/or, worse, without a date, is limited to a mute, raw image. This is how, in turn, the images raised their own questions: Because of the place and time involved, these were not simple. Where, when, how? Who photographed the palaces? Who was there at the time and why did they do it? This is what the present work has attempted to clarify.

Such a study can only follow its material. While theoretically starting in 1860 with the "destruction" of the palaces, the photography begins only in 1873, with the first recorded images; it concludes in 1925, the year Sun Wen (Sun Yat-sen) died, and the dawn of a period of irreversible changes with the end of the so-called "Warlord" period. It transpired that Western photography in China was indeed a field in itself; therefore, no attempt was made to consider Chinese photographic sources.

Prior to discovering the photographers acting in the drama, it was necessary to survey the field: investigating the early and largely ignored manifestations of photography in Imperial Beijing; surveying the walled city the photographers of the European Palaces had lived in; considering the development of photography from the date of the first record of Beijing, how it changed, and how information on its advancement was spread as far away as China. Moving from the means, photography in Beijing, to the object studied, the European Palaces, it became evident that history did not stop with a fire, that ruins also have a history—especially with cameras around—recalling their amazing creation and witnessing their unspeakable devastation.

Figure 2. Pavilion in the center of the Maze, c. 1873, albumen print att. E. Ohlmer

Then came the Western men—yes, men only—who photographed the European Palaces. By some twist of fate they were a pollster's dream: 9 individuals representing 7 countries. They reached, and left, China in the course of 65 years. They included a German sailor, an English gas engineer, a working-class Frenchman, a German nobleman and diplomat, a Berlin-born American architect, a Danish telegraph director, a Finno-Swedish art historian, a Washington archeologist . . . and even a "real" photographer, who made a name in nude photography. They came to China for a variety of reasons, none of which were remotely connected with the European Palaces. For all of them, China was a turning point in their lives and, for most of them, their careers.

This is how, beyond the decaying piles of stones they carefully recorded, the personas of the photographers came to shape the study. While their photographs of the European Palaces are the only clear common ground among them, as a group they embody a long page in the history of photography and of Sino-Western relations.

The research for this book took place between 1987 and 1994, with some additional information later filling in gaps. As most of it was conducted by mail, a review of the letters exchanged brings back the atmosphere and feelings of the time, weeks and months of fruitless search followed by sudden and simultaneous finds that most often launched the researcher in a totally new direction or, more rarely, in retracing her steps. Although each of these stories was amateur detective work, together they were somehow weaving a tapestry: as when working with threads of all colors, one could only guess at what was being produced. The resulting harmony could only come as a surprise.

Time, an enemy of architecture and memories, is also becoming a friend. Awareness of the intrinsic value of photographic archives is spreading throughout the world, improving both indexing of existing resources and conservation methods. Further discoveries should therefore follow this research and contribute to the preservation in memories of the Western "follies" of the Qianlong emperor, and of the men who refused to let them be forgotten.

PART I: PHOTOGRAPHY, BEIJING AND EUROPEAN PALACES

The second half of the nineteenth century will be remembered as a time of technical innovation coupled with intensive colonial expansion. Travel photography belongs to both spheres; steam power shortened distances, armies cleared the way, and photographers recorded images of faraway lands only imagined before. Written descriptions had previously attracted limited attention, but now the reproduction of images made on the spot fostered much greater public interest. Travel magazines and tales of more or less distant peoples and monuments multiplied. Orientalist images of all shapes and descriptions illustrated stories; within a few years of the invention of photography, the medium would become a necessary source of information.

This is the time when Beijing was opened to modern Western visitors. From 1860 on, their presence developed apace with photography, and so did their accounts of Beijing architecture and people. As a consequence, the history of Western life in late imperial and early republican Beijing is also that of a photographic record of the capital.

A well-known, although little photographed, Beijing architectural group, the European Palaces owed much to the outside world; while they would not have been destroyed without the West, without it they would not have been built either, or photographed before they had decayed beyond recognition. The European Palaces are a milestone in the contacts between East and West, and their images are another.

1. EARLY PHOTOGRAPHY IN BEIJING, 1860–1873

Photography was officially born in 1838; four years later, the first of the "Opium Wars" forced China to open five ports to international trade. This is how the new medium and Western presence on the China coast developed simultaneously. Soon, photographic images of the newly accessible empire were found throughout Western albums and publications. What the first photographers recorded in China had a long-lasting influence; it also prepared the ground for the first exposures of the European Palaces in 1873.

EARLY PHOTOGRAPHY IN CHINA

Throughout the centuries, China had often been wary of foreign visitors. In the early nineteenth century, Westerners were fully denied residence in China. Even after the 1842 Treaty of Nanjing, they were only allowed in the open, or "treaty" ports, a handful of coastal towns far from Beijing. This is why, to this day, no photograph of the capital of the Qing empire is dated before the arrival of the French and British troops during the last phase of the China Campaign in October 1860.[1]

This is confirmed by a well-known photographic incident following the signing of the treaty ending the hostilities. As stated by an eyewitness,

> *The indefatigable Signor Beato [. . .] directed the large lens of the camera full against the breast of the unhappy Prince Kung (Gong). The royal brother looked up in a state of terror, pale as death* (Knollys 1875, 209–10).

Obviously the technique, or at least the camera, was still unknown to the emperor's brother. (Sadly, this history-making exposure came to nothing for lack of light.)

By then, however, photographers were already very active in Hong Kong, as well as in treaty ports like Canton, Shanghai and Fuzhou. The Frenchman Jules Itier had made daguerreotypes in Macao and in Whampoa on the Canton estuary in 1844–45,[2] and a photographic studio had been advertised in the Hong Kong *China Mail* as early as 8 October 1846.[3] In 1858, Canton had been seized by Franco-British troops and occupied. This had opened the city to a professional photographer sent by the London firm of Negretti & Zambra, who made the first commercial stereographs of China. He was M. Rossier, a Frenchman.[4]

Figure 3. China in the nineteenth century.

All kinds of photographers were at work in China. Some belonged to the military. In 1855, the British regiment of the Royal Engineers had started training field photographers, a practice soon emulated by other regiments. Besides the commissioned work, the military counted amateur photographers among their ranks. Still, the golden opportunity to photograph China as it was being opened to the world was limited to a few ports, and not always successful. In 1858, the negative plates made in Tianjin by R. Morrison during Lord Elgin's first mission to China, probably the first photographs ever made in that part of the world, were lost in an accident to the luggage (*PN*, 14 January 1859, 221). Likewise, if the French plenipotentiary ambassador, Baron Gros, a keen daguerreotypist, used his skills in China between 1858 and 1861, that work has been lost.

Among the professionals active in south China during the early years, Felice Beato is the best known, because of his work during the China Campaign. In addition, the Hong Kong photographer Milton Miller made a number of individual or group portraits of officers (see album C779 H345, PEM). He also produced very attractive and sensitive portraits of Chinese.[5]

RESEARCHING EARLY PHOTOGRAPHY IN CHINA

In fact, foreign photographers active in China during the nineteenth century were soon forgotten. While scattered research has taken place over the last twenty-five years, the fragmentary results are still a long way from giving a complete picture of Western photography in Imperial China.

Methodology is one of the problems. As in other disciplines of the history of art, the identification of works by historians of photography relies on their author and the aesthetic quality of the prints. However, the method is particularly unsuited to the study of early photography in China, where most prints are anonymous and of poor quality. As a consequence the material held in specialized collections tends to be limited and repetitive.

Actually, the first criteria of selection for a nineteenth century traveler was the documentary value of the image. The photographer's name was not recorded—if the seller ever even knew it. When this study started in 1987, Felice Beato and John Thomson were the only nineteenth century photographers whose work in north China had been extensively studied. Things have not changed much in the intervening years. Antoine Fauchery, Ernst Ohlmer, Théophile Piry, Alfons Mumm von Schwarzenstein and the other photographers found along the road to the European Palaces are still awaiting recognition.

A first important step in the study of early photography in China was the publication by Worswick and Spence (1978, 150–1) of a list of photographers active in China. The list needs to be corrected and added to extensively, but remains at this time the only published research of its kind. In addition, an enormous inventory of photographers and photographs must take place worldwide before serious studies in the field can be undertaken.

A few photographers' images of China have been studied, their work being preserved as a whole and identified. This is the case for Jules Itier (Gimon 1981) and John Ashton Papillon (Falconer 1982). Beato and Thomson are extensively covered because their own commercial approach makes it possible to trace their work. But the activities of M. Miller, L.F. Fisler, W. Saunders, and H.C. Cammidge, well-established photographers in Hong Kong and Shanghai between 1860 and 1885, are still undocumented (even, for most, as to their full names). Their work is found at random, anonymous, among masses of albums and bundles of documentary photographs or portraits assembled by the original purchaser. Experience shows that studying the artistic content of nineteenth century photography in China will only be possible when a sufficient inventory and a suitable data bank become available.

Obstacles are many. They include the scattering of material among public or private repositories too diverse for organized research. The collections themselves are seldom recorded, indexing is rare and often erroneous, sometimes even as to the country shown! As a result, major historical sources have been overlooked and false information on late Imperial China published.[6]

The few studies available on early photography in China are also limited to the open ports, and/or to later years. The only general studies were published by Capa (1972), Beers (1978), Goodrich and Cameron (1978), Marbot and Viénet (1978), and Worswick and Spence (1978)—five titles in all. This is pitiful compared with similar research on the Middle East or Japan. Furthermore, the last of these works was published in 1978.

This is why photography in Beijing before 1900 is still *terra incognita*. Old-fashioned exploration has its rewards: it was a pleasant surprise to see several early portfolios surface during the search for photographs of the European Palaces.

THE CHINA CAMPAIGN OF 1860

Photographs of the China Campaign of 1860 became part of this study on the assumption that the photographers present at the Rape of the Summer Palace would have left images: they were, in any case, the only ones who could have done so during the twelve days between the beginning of the sacking and the fire. Ultimately, this trail did not yield any view of the European Palaces, but provided a number of new images and documents on the early recording of Beijing.

In 1860, photography was still a noteworthy activity, and it is attested that several photographers followed the French and British armies with their equipment. One of them, Lieutenant John Ashton Papillon, a Royal Engineer, produced impressive images between Canton and the Dagu forts on the Beihe river.[7] But he fell sick and was evacuated one month later on 29 September; he was apparently not replaced in his photographic duties. In fact, only two photographers can be identified in Beijing in 1860, Antoine Fauchery and Felice Beato, who were respectively with the French and the British armies during most of the Campaign.

Antoine Fauchery (1823–1861)

Beyond his importance for the history of photography, Antoine Fauchery's case highlights the general shortcomings of French contemporary sources in matters in any way related to the Summer Palace and its deplorable fate.

While his work in China has not been formally identified, there are two potential sources: an anonymous set of twenty-four stereoscopic images of the French army in Canton, Shanghai, Tianjin and Beijing, as well as a view of the Beijing cathedral made on 29 October on the occasion of the *Te Deum* service celebrating the victory.[8] The whole subject matter is very patriotic, indicating a probable French work, and the author of at least the stereoscopic set appears to be Antoine Fauchery.

The photographic records of the Campaign had been eagerly anticipated in France. The Société Française de Photographie received word that three photographers were marching with the armies: Lieutenant-Colonel Du Pin (or Dupin), head of the army's topographical department, Mr. Legrand, a French photographer established in Shanghai,[9] and Antoine Fauchery, correspondent for *Le Moniteur Universel* (*BJP* 8, 15 January 1861, 38). However, no record of the photographic activities in Beijing of the first two are found in military archives, campaign accounts or the history of photography.

Fauchery was already experienced when he was attached in Shanghai to the French army's topographical bureau as an official photographer. In 1858–59, he had been one of the first professional photographers in Melbourne, Australia (Reilly and Carew 1983, 13–17).[10] A friend of Nadar, he had previously made a name in Paris as a journalist, theater and travel writer, cartoonist and sketcher. Living in Australia between 1852 and 1859, he had been in turn a gold digger, grocer, café owner and photographer. Setting off for the Philippines in February 1859, he acquired a passport for China in Manilla in March 1860 (Reilly and Carew 1983, 17). He was in Shanghai at the end of June 1860, and died in April 1861 in Yokohama, Japan. His photographic work in East Asia has not been identified. While it is clear that he went to Beijing with the army as an "official photographer," as yet no view of China can safely be credited to him.

His very activities are unclear. The only official source, the military archives, recorded his progress in China only from 30 June to 7 September 1860.[11] He then vanished from the records. The fact that even his leaving the army went unrecorded is very irregular. However, many events occurred between 5 and 14 October. During those nine days, against all regulations, no orders were registered by the headquarters of this 7,000 man army. Incidentally—or, perhaps, not so incidentally—the Summer Palace was taken and looted between 6 and 9 October. Were the looting and Fauchery's "disappearance" connected?

Whoever produced the twenty-four plates was in Beijing on 15 October when the city surrendered. The images show French soldiers on top of the city walls, as well as a crowd restrained by ropes across the "main street leading to the imperial palace," a scene described and sketched on the occasion of the surrender of the town (Wolseley 1862, 307; *ILN* 5 January 1861, 12), and probably repeated for the signing of the treaties a week later. Why, then, is Fauchery not mentioned in the orders, the regular recording of which had resumed on 14 October? There should have been orders suspending his daily stipend, returning his horse, arranging his transportation south, etc. In addition, his articles in *Le Moniteur* do not show any interruption until the last letter dated 4 December. He then stated that he was on board the military transport *Rhône*, sailing south after witnessing the signature of the British and the French treaties on 23 and 24 October. The military archives are mute on all this.

More troubling still, Montauban, the French commander-in-chief, twice bemoaned lacking a photographer on hand, when the Summer Palace was seized on 6 October and for the signing of the French-Chinese treaty in Beijing on the 24th (Cousin-Montauban 1932, 372). The clear implication is that Fauchery was not available, and that neither Du Pin, who was present, nor Legrand, if he ever went north with the army, were able to stand in for him. And while Fauchery's writing may be more hearsay than the eyewitness account it purported to be, a British diplomat mentioned meeting the *Moniteur* correspondent at the Yuanmingyuan on 6 October (Swinhoe 1861, 299–300). On the other hand, the description of the Summer Palace in the "Letters" was extremely fanciful.[12] In particular, the human-shaped sculptures, supposedly found in quantities, do not belong in a Chinese garden where nudity would be a rare obscenity. Were the embellishments added by a Paris editor more familiar with Versailles than with Chinese garden tradition?

The questions remain: When did Fauchery give up his position as an official photographer, when did he leave Beijing, and what did he record? The key to these mysteries will perhaps be found in another set of photographs in the same collection, comprising twenty-five views of Yedo (Tokyo) and Yokohama in Japan. Identical to the China suite, it is certainly the work of the same photographer. The views are exclusively portraits of Japanese and typical scenes or landscapes. In complete contrast to the China series, no Westerner is shown.

In addition, and contrary to those for China, the captions for Japan are vague or erroneous, as if the photographer had not been able to document his work upon sending it to Paris. Fauchery was in Japan only between January 1861 and his death the following April. These Japan spring views might be easier to document than the China ones. If they are Fauchery's, so is the China set. Nonetheless, troubling inconsistencies remain at military level. Even if the Frenchman's deletion from the official records was a retaliation for his writing the first true French account of the looting in the Summer Palace, in direct challenge to Montauban's version of orderly conquest, it was absurd.

Felice (Felix) Beato (ca. 1830–ca. 1906)

The earliest photographs of Beijing which can be credited with certainty are Felice Beato's. An Italian-born civilian of British nationality, Beato was the semi-official photographer of the British army during the China Campaign. His early professional years are still unclear, partly because he was long confused with his brother Antonio, photographer of the Middle East. In any event, it is known that he attached himself to Lord Elgin's British force which left for China in 1857, only to be redirected towards India caught in the Sepoy rebellion. While other photographers were present, Beato's views of the aftermath of the rebellion already displayed what would become his trademark in war photography, dead enemy bodies in the foreground. His views of battlefields certainly validate the 1856 comment in *The Times*, that

> *The photographer who follows in the wake of the modern armies must be content with conditions of repose and with the still life which remains when the fighting is over.*

A military surgeon noted on August 21, 1860 after the battle of the Dagu forts,

> *I passed into the [North Dagu] fort, and a distressing scene of carnage disclosed itself [. . .] Signor Beato was here in great excitement, characterizing the group [of bodies] as "beautiful," and begging that it might not be interfered with until perpetuated by his photographic apparatus, which was done a few minutes afterwards* (Rennie 1862, 112).

Beato was certainly exposing one of his famous views showing dead Chinese soldiers on the foreground. It has even been suggested that Beato moved and added corpses for a better effect: his "still lives" are indeed too beautifully composed to be credited only to chance.

He probably went with the armed forces from India to China in early 1860, and followed them from Hong Kong to Beijing with his equipment and assistants, creating an impressive record of the war. His views of the Campaign are often found together in chronological order, filling whole, carefully captioned albums. He apparently printed his views and sold them to the allied officers along the way.[13]

In 1861, Beato travelled to Japan in the suite of the plenipotentiary ambassador, Lord Elgin. He was back in London at the end of the year, when he left with his agent, H. Hering, a *Collection of Photographic Views and panoramas taken by Signor F. Beato during the Indian Mutiny [. . .] and the late war in China [. . .]* (the "Hering List"). He finally settled in Yokohama, Japan, and continued his remarkable career with a photographic studio he kept until 1877. He had not abandoned war photography, however; he was in Korea with the U.S. China Squadron in 1871 (*NCH* 7 July 1871),[14] and in Sudan with the British army in 1884. He then opened studios in Rangoon and Mandalay in Burma, where he became a determining influence in early photographically illustrated postcards (Singer 1993, 8–9).

Beato is often credited with introducing hand-tinted prints to Japan. Early photography in Japan is indeed famous for the unmatched beauty and delicacy of its colored prints, and Beato largely contributed to the movement and to its quality. However, local artists had been introduced to photography by the Dutch traders from Deshima Island (Nagasaki) even before Commodore Perry's arrival in 1853, and early on they had developed a local style inspired from their traditional woodblock prints and owing little to the West. More precisely, Beato's studio, through his own work and that of his partner and successors, Raimund von Stillfried, Kusakabe Kimbei and Adolfo Farsari, was strongly influential on export photography, and thus on the image of Japan transmitted to the West.

There are thirty-two views of Beijing and its environs in Beato's famous China series of 102 numbers (Hering List), and all were taken in October 1860. Their appeal to contemporaries is attested to by the high percentage they make up in most albums of the Campaign.[15] Some of the views showing the Examination Halls or the Forbidden City from the city walls are panoramas on strips made of several prints pasted end to end, a genre in which he excelled.

His photographs are usually hand captioned on the album page. Six are entitled "Yuen Ming Yuen," but the extension of the name—which rightly applies only to the garden studied here—to a much larger area, was common at the time and at least four of them are outside the Yuanmingyuan proper.[16] This leaves two views by Beato which might possibly show the Yuanmingyuan, one captioned "clock tower," and an airy pavilion.[17] Considering the importance and architectural wealth of the site, half a dozen views of the Summer Palace area, taken between the arrival of the allied troops on the evening of 5 October and the start of the destruction on the 18th, seem a modest production. But Beato's equipment was extremely cumbersome, the troops reached the Yuanmingyuan in a forced march,

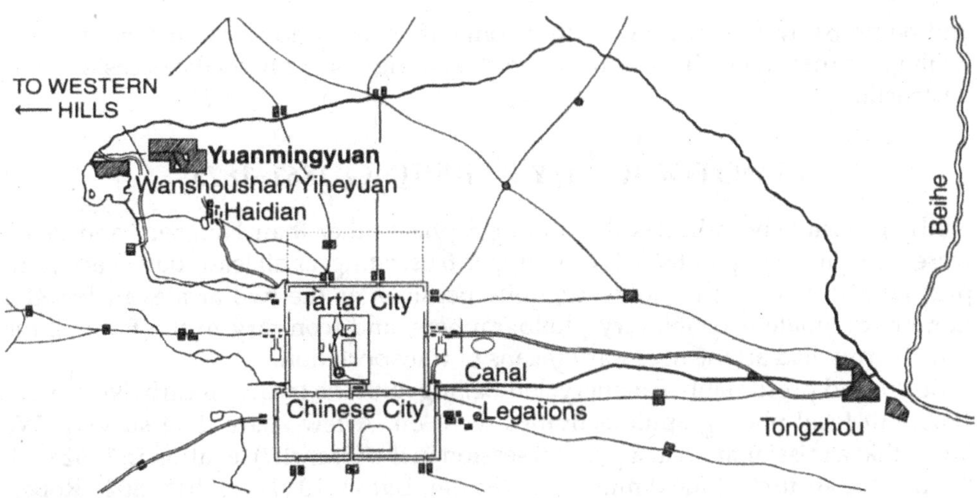

Figure 4. Beijing and the Summer Palace area. Adapted from *The Citizen's Atlas*, London 1895.

Figure 5. Chinese pavilion before the fire, Summer Palace area, October 1860. Engraved from Felice Beato by *The Illustrated London News* (27 April 1861:390).

and he probably caught up with them only after they had retraced their steps to Beijing. He may in fact have gone to the Yuanmingyuan only on the occasion of its destruction.

PHOTOGRAPHY IN BEIJING, 1861–1873

Nothing positively indicates that photographers other than Fauchery and Beato were active in Beijing in 1860. (The search is frustrating, as all leads have very complex ramifications.) It is, however, quite possible, as the two armies included a number of amateur or military photographers, and (contrary to the French) the British army had all the necessary means of transportation.

Beato, and presumably Fauchery, left Beijing with the troops in early November 1860, but local photographic activities went on. A few spare data survive. We know that a missionary had a portrait session in the (French?) legation in 1862 with "two of the six first Chinese ministers" (Favier, *Lettres*, 10 November 1862). Robert Hart, the Inspector General of the Customs, posed in 1864 in pajamas for Albert Brett, one of his student-interpreters (Hart 1991, 158). In the French legation, Paul

Champion and Georges Morache gathered portraits and typical scenes. Images were sometimes shared or published. Most of the engravings illustrating a long article on the Beijing life of the first French minister and his wife were done from photographs (*TDM* 1864:1, 81 n. 1). Among the important works from the early years of Western life in Beijing is also a beautiful series from the early 1860s, probably gathered by a photographer attached to the British legation.[18] In addition, and despite the difficult road, a few tourists brought their equipment to Beijing.

The period from 1861 to 1873 and its related problems can be illustrated with three names: Paul Champion, Georges Morache and John Thomson.

Paul Champion (1838-after 1877)

Paul Champion, a French chemistry engineer and amateur photographer, was in China and Japan in 1865–66. His images received a bronze medal at the 1867 Paris *Exposition Universelle* (World's Fair),[19] and were subsequently reproduced in various publications. Champion used them in his own study of technique and architecture in the official catalogue of the *Exposition*.[20] The Beijing photographs are outstanding, with stunning Chinese scenes; several of them show the same backdrop of bamboo lattice which was probably in a courtyard of the French legation.[21]

Figure 6. Musicians in Beijing (det.) in 1865 by P. Champion, albumen print. (Also found attr. to G. Morache in *Le Tour du Monde* (1876:2, 225).)

Yet Champion the man is quite unknown. Establishing a precise biography would go far beyond the scope of the present work, as there are no photographs of the Yuanmingyuan among the thirty-four images by Champion traced by this research (Appendix 4). However, as one of the first photographers recorded for Beijing, he deserves more than a passing notice. He was one of those scientists who left accounts of a personal experience in East Asia, and his 1867 paper "On the difficulties met in Photography in regions such as China and Japan" is an important reference. A few sources show that Champion was in Beijing in 1865 on some official "mission." Back in Paris in 1866, he became a laboratory assistant at the prestigious Conservatoire National des Arts et Métiers. A pencilled note stating that he had "resigned" is dated 1871.[22]

Champion was a member of the Société Française de Photographie and published several papers in its *Bulletin* between 1860 and 1876; he was also elected editor of the journal in October 1872. His publications dealt with photography, chemistry and his East Asia trip. At the same time, he was also writing about explosives for military use, an interesting connection with gun cotton used in the collodion formula and also an explosive.

The photographer's images of China were used in France by the press and in books. *Le Monde Illustré* (24 May 1868, 122) engraved his view of a Beijing *pailou* (ceremonial arch) for which he wrote a long comment. In 1873, the weekly *L'Illustration* reproduced several of his views of the Chinese capital, without credit, and under circumstances that raise serious questions about Champion and Morache's respective productions.

Georges Morache (1837–1906)

Georges Morache, a military doctor, was attached to the French Legation from 1862 to 1866. While in Beijing, he studied medicine and astronomy. In 1868, under the dry title of *Beijing and its population, hygiene studies,* he published interesting research on Chinese mode of life in Beijing.

In 1876, *Le Tour du Monde* credited Morache with a series of sixty photographs illustrating a long article by T. Choutzé [*alias* Gabriel Devéria], "Beijing and North China." The images included thirty-two views of architecture and eleven portraits of Chinese or Westerners. Typical scenes, including small trades or types of Chinese, made up one-third of the images. It appeared at first glance that, either as a doctor or from personal interest, Morache had easy contacts with the population; hence, one could believe, the high percentage of typical scenes, a minor genre in Beijing photography.

However, this first conclusion was soon tempered by another series credited to Morache. In the Musée de l'Homme in Paris were a further sixty images, of which only thirty-nine were found in *Le Tour du Monde*. They were early prints on albumen paper including a number of typical scenes, but the proportion of types of Chinese and of Beijing monuments was significantly higher.[23] In addition, as is often the case, what was printed did not quite agree with what could be documented. As John Thomson's work is probably the best documented for East Asia, it was easy to see that a few of the "Morache" views engraved in *Le Tour du Monde* were his.

One would have thought the 1876 attribution by Devéria to be a reference, since himself, Morache and quite certainly Champion, all lived in the Beijing legation at the same time. But in fact, he is partly responsible for Morache and Champion's works being intermingled to an extraordinary extent. This is the second, and major, problem.

The only images clearly attributed to Morache are found in *Le Tour du Monde* (engravings) and the Musée de l'Homme (prints), for a total of eighty-one views.[24] Unfortunately, neither source is high quality. Engravings as a rule retain only the central subject, while the prints were not originals, but copies. This is all the more regrettable because eight of Morache's Beijing views are also found in Champion's portfolio. The latter images, sharper and much larger, are certainly originals; for these eight at least, Champion, not Morache, should have been named as the photographer.

A few "engravings from photographs" published by *L'Illustration* in Paris on 13 September 1873 further complicate the matter. Without giving any credit, they seem to borrow from both sources. The portraits, found in the Morache collection, may have been produced in a studio, most probably not in Beijing. The Musée de l'Homme recorded them as "Manchuria," which is also a puzzle, as one of them purportedly shows the son of the military governor of Beijing and his wife.

There are further involvements. Champion's cobbler is not the same man as Morache's. The toy peddler from *L'Illustration* belongs to neither and could be an engraver's creation. The group of musicians in *Le Tour du Monde,* captioned as Thomson's and found in the Morache collection, is by Champion. And, finally, was Morache even a photographer, or was he simply a collector?

John Thomson (1837–1920)

The first professional photographer well documented in Beijing after 1860 is John Thomson, a Scotsman prominent in the development of illustrated travel literature. After photographing Cambodia, Thomson had in 1868 set up a studio in Hong Kong, where he produced standard commercial photography. There are *Cartes de visite* photographs bearing on the back his stamp, "J THOMSON PHOTOGRAPHER," some of them captioned at length with an explanation of the scene, and/or colored, which is unusual.[25] *The China Magazine* of Hong Kong also used his work in 1868–69. Hong Kong was the base from which Thomson travelled to Formosa (Taiwan) and inland China between 1868 and 1872.

The 1873–74 publication of the four volumes of his masterpiece, *Illustrations of China and its People,* met with well-deserved success. The two hundred prints are high quality calotypes, thirty-seven of them on Beijing and environs.[26] However, and just like Beato, Fauchery and Champion, Thomson failed to leave views of the European Palaces of the Yuanmingyuan.

As all of Thomson's work, his photographs of China show a rare sensitivity to people's lives. Portraits and typical scenes abound, showing the life of ordinary people as well as that of the aristocrat or the merchant. Thomson was exceptional for his time in his dealings with the Chinese. Race was irrelevant to him in a time and place where Westerners and Chinese had no intercourse barring that of necessity. He wrote very naturally of them, leaving his reader to wonder whether the

Figure 7. "Mandarin Yang", an amateur photographer in his Beijing courtyard in 1871 by John Thomson. *Illustrations of China and its People*, IV:14.

"friend" mentioned here or there was Chinese or Western. Obviously, this extraordinary attitude opened to him doors which usually remained closed to foreign photographers.

On occasion, the Scotsman's inquisitiveness found him in delicate situations. Such incidents were often connected to a local and long-lasting belief: that foreigners were "buying up little children, whose flesh they eat, and whose eyes they use for photographic purposes" (Hart 1991, 149).[27] The buying part refers to the custom of missionaries to give some money to people who brought them orphans to raise. The connection between eyes and photography was logical; considering the volatility of a Chinese mob, it was also very dangerous.

*
* *

To counter the difficulty of practicing photography in China in the first decades, the treaty port professional photographers usually worked in their studios or at least far from the crowds. Generally, the limited selection of topics may be explained by personal safety concerns as much as by racial prejudice. Also, in Beijing, Chinese reticence was a factor in limiting the early coverage of Chinese life to buildings.

The work of professional photographers is hard to credit and to date, partly due to the short average duration of their stay in China. Research becomes even more difficult when dealing with amateurs. The quality of their work was usually in line with the professionals', but it enjoyed only a limited distribution in China and abroad and was rarely signed or credited. Except for albums kept in family archives, their history is little known.

Otherwise, as with so many fields in the second half of the nineteenth century, the distinction between "professional" and "amateur" in photography is vague. Many photographers later considered professionals, came to the technique while pursuing other careers. A few "amateurs" also left a production important at both photographic and documentary level. One of the photographers of the Yuanmingyuan, Thomas Child, worked as a gas engineer throughout his productive years as a photographer of Beijing. It is generally accepted that a photographer is professional when he routinely sells his work, whether or not the images are published by other people. In this respect, Paul Champion was clearly an amateur, while Child was a professional. But in the end, each, in his own way, was an important early photographer of Beijing.

2. FOREIGNERS IN BEIJING, 1860–1925

> *It is a special blessing for a China resident to have a Hobby. A good active absorbing hobby, that engrosses his attention and carries him out of himself at a canter . . .* (*NCH*, 31 August 1872).

The walled city of Beijing was the meeting point of the photographers of the European Palaces. All lived in the capital; some remained in China for decades. This was certainly a factor in their interest in the architecture of the capital. One wonders, in fact, about the way of life of a Westerner in the Beijing of old, and of the role of photography in his daily routine. In other words, "How did a photographer of the European Palaces live in Beijing?"

When the first series on the European Palaces was shot in the nineteenth century, Beijing was a world apart offering foreigners a unique mode of life. Making a photograph there required much deliberation and organization. In 1877, Thomas Child spent whole days with his servants in expeditions to the Yuanmingyuan which were planned and prepared several days in advance. In 1915, when Carl Whiting Bishop hailed rickshaws and undertook to record the sights of the city between visits and errands, he could rightly claim after less than four weeks to have photographed "most of the points of interest in Peking and its immediate vicinity" (Bishop to G.B. Gordon, 28 August 1915, UMA). Forty years earlier, it had taken Child several years to achieve the same result.

THE WALLED CITY OF BEIJING

When the Westerners arrived in 1860, they found what resident seventeenth and eighteenth centuries missionaries had described, but which had rarely been since: several cities enclosed within a series of thick walls. The Forbidden City, the imperial residence where affairs of state were conducted, was surrounded by the Imperial City, then by the Tartar City. To the south stood the Chinese City. Each city was walled, with gates providing access between them or to the suburbs. Most foreigners settled in the Tartar City, south-east of the Forbidden City, in what later became known as the Legations Quarter.

Beijing had been developed on the lines set up in the Ming dynasty, with streets crossing at right angles. Very wide streets were cut by narrower ones, and so on to the many alleys. As usual in China, wealthy houses opened to the street through gates piercing blind walls, beyond which buildings spread around a sequence of courtyards.

The Tartar and Chinese cities had been designed to keep conquering and conquered populations apart. By 1860, however, this was no longer strictly enforced, and Manchus (or "Tartars") and Chinese mingled to some extent. The early photographic views of Beijing show the streets and their *pailou*, the Imperial City with its marble bridges and lakes, the Bell tower and the Drum Tower from which were sounded the hours and the signal to open or close the city gates, and numerous temples, including the Temple of Heaven where the Emperor worshiped his ancestors. All these monuments were dominated by the vast city walls and their towering gates.

South of Hatamen and Qianmen, two of the gates leading to the Chinese city, an important trading and shopping area was often photographed from the walls. Qianmen was a major point of passage between the Tartar and Chinese cities, but its central door was reserved for use by the Emperor. All day long, the lateral doors saw the passage of traders and travellers riding carts, donkeys, camels, chairs, wheelbarrows, or simply walking. Images show the lines of horse carts waiting for hire in the middle of the street, the numerous open-air restaurants where a bowl of noodles could be had at any time of day or night, and the white marble "Beggars' Bridge" over the moat. The tall gilded fronts of the shops concealed cavernous mazes where, from courtyard to courtyard, desirable patrons were led to peruse the best merchandise. This was also the entertainment quarter, with its open-air and indoor theaters.

Figure 8. Beggar's Bridge seen from Qianmen (near the Legation Quarter), 1865. Engraving from ph. by P. Champion, here attr. to G. Morache (*Le Tour du Monde* (1876:2, 197).)

Then there were the people. The few street scenes photographed during the first years show a vast diversity of population, and considerable activity. Crowds were everywhere, peddlers and beggars, noblemen and soldiers, merchants and carters, Chinese and Manchu. The men all wore the queue or pigtail, which laborers rolled around their head when working to keep it out of the way. Few women of quality were seen, although Manchu noblewomen, who could walk unhindered by bound feet, enjoyed more freedom than Chinese ladies. They wore long embroidered robes and high butterfly-like headdresses ornamented with real or jewelled flowers. Ladies traveled in carts for privacy, servants carrying out errands for their mistresses.

Beijing was very hot and wet for a few weeks in summer and bitterly cold in winter. Photographs show the seasons by the clothing worn. The date when officials switched from summer to winter wear was fixed by imperial edict and followed by the people. Cold weather also saw the return of trains of Bactrian camels whose Mongol drivers planted their tents inside the walls close to the legations.

*
* *

As a result of the Treaty of Beijing of 1860, the only requirement to reach the capital had become a visa issued by a foreign consulate in Tianjin; Chinese authorities could not prevent the movements of a passport-carrying Westerner. However, Beijing did not become a tourist attraction until the late nineteenth century because for a long time its only recognized appeal lay in its monuments and its proximity to the Great Wall. What the legendary walls of Beijing had long been hiding had finally been revealed in October 1860, and it had been a general disappointment. The city was filthy, "in ruins" (clearing off damaged buildings was prohibited by law), the streets full of refuse and so rutted they were barely passable even when unflooded, and the stench was overpowering. In addition, beggars were as repulsive as they were plentiful and crowds hostile, or at best annoyingly curious.

Those foreigners who still came, often brought with them the preconceived and civilizing ideas of the imperialist West. They deprecated everything that was not progress, that is, a society based on modern Western values. Authentic interest for the real China was the exception. In all things, Westerners preferred the company of their kind to that of the Chinese, whose language they rarely understood. Their contempt was fully shared by the Chinese, who paid as little attention as possible to their "barbarian" guests. The initial visitors generated the dual image of a China begging for progress and of the civilizing influence of Europeans, which was so prevalent in the West in the late nineteenth century.[1]

WESTERN LIFE IN BEIJING

For years, foreign powers had labored for the privilege of maintaining permanent missions in the capital of China, and it was considered an important concession when it was finally granted in 1860. Immediately after the war, Russia opened the first legation, while Catholic and Protestant missionaries from Europe and the United States began to settle in the city. French and British diplomats followed in

March 1861. By 1874, Austria-Hungary, France, Germany, Great Britain, Italy, the Netherlands, Russia, Spain and the United States were all represented in Beijing, by a total of forty-six men.[2] The Western secular community was completed by a Russian at the observatory, seven professors at the Tongwenguan, the new college created to train Chinese diplomats in international relations, and thirteen men with the Customs—the body which produced the photographers.

The 1860 treaty had not opened Beijing to foreign trade. The first foreign shop was permitted to open only in 1874, after years of requests from the diplomats, and still in 1889, *The Chronicle and Directory*[3] listed under "Professions, trades, &c." only six names in all, and a total Western non-missionary population of a hundred and one (plus seventy-eight missionaries), all on three pages. By that time, the oldest legation had been in Beijing twenty-nine years. In contrast, the directory granted the port of Tianjin seven pages, and thirty-nine to Shanghai.

The daily life of Westerners in Beijing was quite different from that in Shanghai or other treaty ports, although there were significant similarities. As a rule, resident foreigners made no concession to the climate or other local conditions, and they tried to maintain their usual way of life. In the south, eating and drinking habits added to unsuitable clothing to contribute to a heavy mortality rate, but Beijing was considered healthy.

Shanghai, being an international center, had a real cultural life, with newspapers in several languages, learned societies, theater, clubs, racecourse and parties. The membership list of the famous Asiatic Society was a prime example of internationalism (but not of universalism since, of course, no Chinese was invited to join).[4] In contrast, even from a Chinese point of view, Beijing was geographically and culturally isolated, a slow and rather provincial place.

In 1871, it could still be said that "The voyage to Pekin is always a serious business. In the very best weather it takes ten days to go there from Shanghai, and eight to return" (Hübner 1875, 471). This was true until the end of the century, when the railway would considerably shorten the trip. The one-hundred kilometers between Tianjin, the nearest port, and the town of Tongzhou near Beijing was either covered by cart or horse on atrocious roads, or by houseboats. More comfortable, the latter were slower and impracticable in winter when the river was frozen solid. The last leg of the journey, twenty kilometers between Tongzhou and Beijing, used the road, which meant spending the better part of a day in a bumpy cart.

Symbolically important to the Western powers, the capital was still nothing more than the place of residence of a small group of their nationals who were allowed to remain on sufferance, aliens cut off from their reluctant hosts by mutual prejudice and customs. The community was a very small world indeed, in which people were interdependent out of necessity.

Most of the men were young and single, a number of them student-interpreters assigned to the legations or the Inspectorate General of the Customs to study Chinese. While it was an exaggeration to write that "as a residence [. . .] Pekin is simply a hell" (Hübner 1875, 513), life was rather familial and uneventful. Lodgings here were quite different from the airy colonial houses built in the treaty ports. The first legations in Beijing settled in Chinese palaces with numerous courtyards, and the Customs followed suit. As a result, the single men had individual apartments and common rooms arranged around interior courtyards. Each of them employed servants, with a "boy" in charge of household shopping.

Figure 9. The Fire Brigade at the British Legation in the 1870s by T. Child. Albumen print.

The gardens of the British and French legations, or those of the Inspectorate General, were pleasant and extensive. Local nurseries provided the potted plants characteristic of Chinese gardens, as well as winter storage in their greenhouses. Seeds were received from home. Yet, while fruit, vegetables, poultry and other staples were cheaper in Beijing than in the coastal towns, everything else had to be ordered from Shanghai or home, or, later, from Tianjin.

The monotony of life in Beijing is reflected by D. Rennie (in Beijing 1861–62), A.B. Freeman-Mitford (ca. 1865), G. Devéria (1860s) and W.H. Wilkinson (ca. 1880).[5] In the face of such boredom, one can easily understand how a hobby such as photography could prosper despite the difficulties in procuring and transporting equipment and supplies. Photography was both absorbing and demanding, probably the very reasons for its success.

Whether tourists or residents in China, visitors provided a welcome distraction, and they easily found people willing to show them the city. If not invited to stay at one of the legations, they lodged in temples according to Chinese custom, or in Chinese inns. In 1866, a resident published a first guidebook. Informative on Beijing, *Notes for tourists in the North of China* clearly stated priorities; it thus ranked the French legation first as to extent and taste, and its "wire-netted enclosure" for live kitchen animals was detailed more fully than most Chinese monuments (Dennys 1866, repr. in Mayers 1867, 515).

Young men escorted visitors to the Great Wall several days away, and to Mongolia. Such excursions required a travelling retinue. One took, for each foreigner, "a man to look after clothes, bedding, and things in general, a cook, and a groom; but besides this our people took with them *their* servant" (Freeman-Mitford, 129). Food was brought along, even tea: village inns outside the main roads supplied "only the pot and the boiling water."

In Beijing, freedom of access to the various sites of the capital fluctuated over the years, often because of foreign misbehavior.[6] In 1865, a young British *attaché* noted that:

> *There is little temptation to travellers to come here now, for, thanks to the misbehaviour of our countrymen, the Chinese have shut the principal lions of the town, and the temples of Heaven, and of Confucius, are not shown, even to members of the Legations* (Freeman-Mitford, 118).

However, walking on the top of the wall surrounding the Tartar City was a favorite exercise. It was easily accessible from the Legations Quarter and the ground was better there than anywhere else. As was often the case in China, this was forbidden in theory, but actually tolerated as long as the Westerners were discreet. The complete circuit around the Tartar City took six hours and offered a series of striking views. In particular, extensive city gardens invisible beyond their walls were revealed, islands of nature offering a pleasant contrast to the deep grey of the brick walls and the colored glazed roof tiles.

Excursions into the city were more problematic. Whatever the conveyance, the going was slow in Beijing. Traffic problems were generated in great part by the disastrous condition of the unpaved streets. Distances were significant, gates closed at sunset, and transportation was primitive. In Beijing, sedan chairs were reserved

No.171. PEKING CARRIAGE

The principal mode of travelling all over the North of China is by such conveyances, for long journeys two [illegible], tandem fashion. This picture shows a good one of its kind such as is used by Mandarins, they take the place of cabs, [illegible] many thousands ply for hire all over the City. The bottom is level, and the passenger has to sit inside cross legged or else [illegible] on the shafts which is the easiest mode of riding, though not so respectable: there being no springs to the vehicle, and the [illegible] streets being of the worst kind, a ride in a Peking carriage is not all pleasure [illegible] one gets used to it in time.

Figure 10. "Beijing Cart" before 1878, by T. Child. Albumen print with a captioning slip.

for high ranking officials, which left as only passenger vehicle the "Peking cart." This was a small, covered and springless horse-drawn cart, where one could only sit cross-legged or lie on a mattress; its inborn lack of comfort allied to the state of roads and streets made a deep impression on anyone who ever used it.

Nevertheless, outings beyond the city gates were frequent. A racecourse set up by the British army in 1860 remained in service. The residents had race meetings with their sturdy mongol ponies, to the great enjoyment of the Chinese crowds who came to watch the peculiar antics of the Westerners.

Among the popular day trips was the imperial park of Wanshoushan north-west of Beijing, still splendid despite extensive damage inflicted during the sack of 1860. The nearby Western Hills were also a privileged place for outings and vacations. Many spent the few weeks of oppressive heat in rented temple courtyards, taking with them furniture, house staff (including their private Chinese tutor), and food for the duration. In 1866, when Freeman-Mitford and a friend went to the Hills for a spell, they took with them "fourteen carts full of every kind of movable—our whole poultry-yard clucking and cackling out of coops and baskets, and a cow with her calf." They were eight hours on the road to cover seventy *li*, about thirty-five kilometers (Freeman-Mitford 1900, 331).

Professional duties were light in Beijing, except perhaps for the students who spent several hours a day on their studies and for the Customs personnel. In fact, many diplomats had very little to do. Thus social life was crucially important, especially for the few ladies who were mainly housebound out of necessity. Everyone subscribed to the library, and sports (tennis, ice skating, bowling, cricket, etc.) were practiced in one or the other of the legations.

Teas, dinners, amateur theatricals, musical and dancing evenings followed upon one another without pause in a life that offered a few peculiarities. Ladies were booked for dancing prior to the evening even being planned so that all men could have a turn (Wilkinson 1885, 152). In 1865, Robert Hart decided to stop drinking champagne or milk with each meal, which seems to imply that, before, he had! (Hart 1991, 311). He was later famous for his garden parties enlivened by his own Chinese brass band. More standard was the British envoy Frederick Bruce (in Beijing 1861–65), ordering his hampers from the luxury grocer Fortnum & Mason in London (Account book, Elgin Papers).

Occasionally, one comes across accounts and mixed reviews of Chinese theater: Chinese gongs did not go well with Western ears. Gabriel Devéria (1876:2, 232–5) enjoyed Chinese food, but Wilkinson (1885, 86) left a disgusted account of the dinner he hosted for his Chinese-language teacher; besides the food (he had selected a Mongol restaurant, possibly not the best choice for the uninitiated), handling chopsticks was simply beyond him. He spent the evening drinking the brandy he had brought, leaving to his Chinese guests the care of ordering the feast he was buying them.

Life changed little over the first decades. In 1875, the exchange of mail with Europe still took five months in summer and was interrupted in winter; however, the Customs maintained a daily service with the icebound port of Tianjin. A French hotel opened, but the rooms may not have been a great improvement over the roadside Chinese inns (Thomson 1898, 245). Between 1865 (Freeman-Mitford) and 1880 (Wilkinson), the only noticeable difference was the size of the community which had doubled with the opening of new legations. Nevertheless, at less than a hundred, the group remained too small for significant changes to occur.

The barrier between the small Western circle and the Chinese was as solid as ever. The two worlds met only when necessary, and very rarely privately. The strict separation may be the reasons for the fame of one "Mandarin Yang," probably the first Chinese photographer in the capital, and a rare individual who sought out Western contacts. He was photographed by John Thomson (Fig. 7,) and described by many; he seems to have been visited by travelers as a rare example of an "enlightened" Chinese.

Yang was identified as Yang Lao Yeh, mandarin of the blue button (third grade) by purchase, owner of numerous pawnshops and sitting on the Board of War, and who lived in the Chinese city at Xijiao Hutong (Magpie Alley): "He has a room fitted up after our fashion, and his house is full of guns, telescopes, clocks, barometers, thermometers, and other foreign importations. He has even gone so far as to fit up a photographic studio, and takes lessons in the art, which he practices with

Figure 11. Coal-laden camels and streetcar tracks in Qianmen Street, 1920s, by G. von Estorff. *Atlantis* (February 1931:84.)

considerable success. He gave us really capital portraits of himself of his own execution . . . " Very thoughtfully, he used to provide his Western guests with forks, to save them from struggling with chopsticks (Freeman-Mitford 1900, 229–37). He remained popular with the foreigners for a long time: "The master of the house was fond of electricity, and kept a battery to light his pipe. He was a photographer too, and took portraits of wife no. 1, in her grandest state dress (Brooks 1872, 196–8). "Mr. Yang studies chemistry, anatomy [. . .] He is in China the first native who used gas lighting [. . .] As he allowed us to make a photograph . . . " (Devéria 1876:2, 240). Was the visitor-photographer John Thomson? Thomas Child, one of the photographers of the Yuanmingyuan, worked for Yang, and probably installed his gas lighting (Osman 24 August 1989, 14).

The opening of the Tianjin-Beijing railway line in 1896, followed in 1900 by the erection of the railway station inside the city walls, was to end forever the isolation of the Western community in Beijing. While early twentieth century visitors to Beijing could never forget they were in China, many amenities of modern life soon became available to them. Railroad, electricity, streetcars, Western architecture—all came within the walls and spread beyond the old Legations Quarter. There was, in fact, a fine balance of comfort and exoticism to be enjoyed. Open-minded Westerners and progressive Chinese had enough in common to meet socially. Indeed, some Westerners became so appreciative of Chinese traditions they "went native," adopting in the old Chinese houses the way of life many modern Chinese were relinquishing (see Kates 1988). With them at least, China had performed her usual feat of conquering her conquerors, at the same time as Chinese men were cutting off their queue and fewer women looked like bright butterflies.

Perversely, just as the Chinese were embracing modern ways, the visitors started to produce evocative images and descriptions of the mode of life their predecessors had contributed to endangering. Scenes of daily life were sympathetically recorded. Temple fairs, weddings and funerals, peddlers, old men airing their singing birds, traditional costumes and customs, were thoroughly photographed and described.[7] Beijing was changing for ever, but its past would not be forgotten.

3. PRACTICING PHOTOGRAPHY IN CHINA, 1860–1925

Pictures of one sort or another [. . .] have come to be a recognized necessity of modern life. ("Some Chinese Pictures" 1869)

For all its crucial importance in the image revolution, photography was not easy to use in its first decades. Each negative, each print, were submitted to lengthy manipulations, with results always uncertain. Between the first made-on-the-spot collodion glass negative plates of the European Palaces of 1873 and the industrial silver gelatin rollfilm of 1915, there is a whole world to explore. Once cumbersome cameras shrank into small boxes, and mechanics and optics followed suit. How photographers worked, and how they managed to do it in China, go a long way towards explaining the images that reached us.

THE PROCESSES

By 1860, when the allied armies brought photography to Beijing, the general principles of modern photography were already set.[1] With a dark chamber and a lens, the photographer made a glass negative which could be printed in quantity. It was a far cry from the first works on salted paper (calotype) by William Henry Fox-Talbot in 1840. The famous daguerreotype was still used, but its principle of single copy condemned it to early oblivion. Thus, photography in China spread almost entirely through "modern" processes. Wet collodion or silver gelatin glass plates were the direct ancestors of today's black and white film.

The photographic history of the European Palaces started in 1873, with wet collodion, as daguerreotype and salted paper were already obsolete. A reliable process going back to the early 1850s, wet collodion's excellent definition allowed it to remain in universal use for over a quarter of a century despite its delicate and cumbersome use, and to last until well after the advent of more sensitive industrial plates.

Details on the wet collodion formula found in the photographic publications of the time are only a reference. Photographers routinely experimented with the basic formulas or added their own components (collodion is a solution of gun cotton in ether and alcohol.) The whole procedure was delicate, most mishaps apparently related to mixing components and coating the plate, or to incorrect exposure time; experience and practice made the good photographer. "Resolute and untiring perseverance" were required, as "failures form an overwhelming majority of [experienced photographers'] earliest and even later efforts."[2] However, in 1873 Beijing, it was probably more difficult to procure the raw material than to find the time to practice one's technique.

A photographic session at the Yuanmingyuan would have started at home in the city, with careful cleaning and other preparation of the glass plates, as well as mixing of the collodion base. The expedition included a few servants to help carry the equipment and provisions for the day, and the horses started out early in the morning. Once on location, the tripod camera was planted in front of the selected subject, and the portable darkroom/laboratory set up close by. The palace or pavilion was first framed and focused, and the occasional live participant warned to hold the pose. Then, the coating of the plate began in the darkroom (pouring the emulsion on the glass in a thin even layer was tricky), followed by drainage of the excess liquid. The plate was sensitized in a chemical bath, set in a closed holder, and carried to the camera. It was exposed by removing the lens cap for the number of seconds giving the proper exposure; light being bright in Beijing, this would rarely have extended to minutes. The still wet, exposed plate was then immediately taken back to the darkroom in its holder to be developed, fixed and washed. From coating to development, the procedure allowed only about three minutes, because a drying emulsion lost its sensitivity. Once dry, careful storage ensured long-lasting conservation of the negatives: the set of wet collodion plates made in 1873 in the Yuanmingyuan by Ohlmer still prints beautifully today.

Printing was done by contact. The very thin albumen-coated paper was sensitized with silver nitrate, then dried. It was squeezed against the negative in a printing frame, to be exposed to daylight for as long as it took to transfer the image, a matter of minutes on a bright day, and considerably longer in dull weather. The finished print was fixed and washed, and often pasted on a stronger support while still wet because it curled into a thin roll when drying. And, all along, the invasive dust of Beijing offered the operator an additional challenge.

About 1874, a new process started a revolution in photography. More sensitive, silver gelatin created instant photography, that is, the clear image of movement. The emulsion was used dry and could be manufactured industrially. From then on, practitioners only had to carry their cameras. The plates, small, thin, and therefore light, were inserted in loading chambers beforehand, to be loaded in the camera in daylight. Sensitivity was foreseeable and reliable; the negative could wait for development, even until the traveller's return from an East Asia trip.

Next came a progressive change from glass to rollfilm. Celluloid and paper film were offered by George Eastman in the United States, and became common with the portable camera. The "pocket" Kodak cameras (1895) consisted of a mere box held on the chest. A convenience to travellers, some cameras offered exchangeable loading chambers for either glass or rollfilm. By that time, silver gelatin printing paper had began supplanting albumen paper.

Simultaneously, the first industrial process of color photography, the autochrome of the brothers Louis and Auguste Lumière, became available in 1907. However, it was slow and required long exposure times. Like modern slides, the

Figure 12. Outdoor shooting session and equipment with the wet collodion process. From *Le Magasin Pittoresque* (1863:389.)

Figure 13. The Pirys and friends at the "Princess' Tomb" on the Tongzhou canal near Beijing, c. 1904. Silver gelatin stereoscopic glass negative by A.T. Piry. Nalka Piry rides the horse, her mother stands behind. The stereoscopic camera seen on the left is the type used by the photographer.

glass plates became positive on development. The autochromes were not meant for printing, but their hues were very soft and aged well.

PHOTOGRAPHIC LITERATURE

Complicated as it was, photography in the years 1860–1895 was limited to a very motivated elite who necessarily acquired a strong basic knowledge of chemistry and optics. Specialized journals, which appeared throughout the world immediately after photography was born, allowed knowledge to be communicated and perfected as far away as China. They also underlined the preeminence of the scientific over the documentary in early photographic experiments: for decades, artistic qualities were only a minor consideration. At the same time, public interest in photography was such that "references to the process turn[ed] up in scientific and literary journals alike" (Sennett 1987, 6).

The proliferation of photographic societies was epidemic in the Western world: by 1890, there were one hundred eleven societies in Great Britain alone (*Year-Book . . . ,* 1891). The societies published bulletins, sometimes jointly. In addition to their own members' contributions, the bulletins translated and abstracted from competitors. Circulation of information was fast, innovative articles spreading worldwide in the space of a few months through specialized magazines as well as general readership publications.

For the period 1860–1925, relevant sources are the journals published by photographic societies, the specialized books and periodicals for photographers, and the non-specialized books and periodicals presenting regular or occasional articles on photography. Also deserving special mention are the periodicals in China which used photography as a direct means of illustration.

The photographic society journals presented their members' activities, with readers' forums commenting on former issues. Optics was much less represented than chemistry, open to all experiments. The field was boundless; there were numerous variations of formulas for printing, enlarging or reducing, many accounts of experiments in color or wet collodion formulas (depending on climate, equipment used, desired effect, etc.). Seasoned and experimental techniques were used concurrently, readers detailing their experiments, commenting on results, and generating lively exchanges.

In 1890, France had sixteen publications exclusively devoted to photography, most of them commercial (*Year-Book* . . . , 1891), combining technical articles and travel accounts.[3] A few titles testify to the rapid specialization of the readership, opening new areas from the history of art to medicine, while almanacs presented articles on novelties in the field as well as advertisements from photographers and suppliers. As many of the latter took mail orders, this was valuable information for expatriate photographers. Equipment manufacturers also regularly published catalogues,[4] and books on photographic technique came under all forms and shapes, from the small booklet to encyclopedias with numerous engraved illustrations. This is how the letters sent from Beijing in 1908–1914 by Théophile Piry, a China resident since 1870, showed a remarkable awareness of materials newly available and of their uses.

In the non-specialized press which published regular or occasional articles on photography, articles were adjusted to the readership. Thus, the delicate problem of artistic property and counterfeits was treated by an art magazine, while travel magazines dealt with photography and travel, or even color photography.[5] This much-covered topic was for a long time the object of research, but its concrete applications had to wait until the advent of autochrome in 1907.

On the China coast, foreign language newspapers were published in the ports open to international trade. They differed little from their Western counterparts and presented the same type of general information on photography.[6]

PUBLISHING PHOTOGRAPHS IN CHINA, 1868–1878

Two China journals are important for the history of photography between 1868 and 1878, as both were illustrated with original photographic prints. Their descriptions of places, essays on local cultures and translations of local literature place them as "travel literature."

The China Magazine (1868–1869) defined its purpose in the first editorial:

> *. . . to publish in Hong Kong a weekly periodical upon the model of the London magazines, but treating subjects relating to China . . .* (18 April 1868, back cover).

There was a need. As stated in Shanghai when the magazine was announced:

> *In effect, photography is the only means by which creditable illustrations can be supplied to illustrate a Chinese periodical. [. . .] Many of us who reside in China, are lammentably [sic] deficient in knowledge of the country, its inhabitants, and their customs . . .* (*NCH* 14 March 1868, 2)[7]

Issue 15 included an article "about composing photos," and until September 1868, John Thomson was in charge of the magazine's photography. Images came with a short description, to which was sometimes added an account of the shooting session. The magazine was of journal size, with prints 9 x 12.5 cm on average. The title folded in its second year.

On 30 May 1870, in Yokohama, John Reddie Black started *The Far East*. Overall, the magazine printed nearly a thousand photographs of China and Japan, several of them by Thomas Child, a Yuanmingyuan photographer. It was to fold at the end of 1878, probably due to the editor's illness which had previously made the publication erratic. "A magazine of the Orient for European eyes," *The Far East* "explored the culture of a country foreign even to the Europeans and Americans who lived there" (White 1991). Articles related to China and Japan, including ongoing photography in which Black had a keen interest. Six albumen paper prints were pasted in each issue, at first inserted in the text, then full page. The images either illustrated the copy or were themselves the object of a short comment.

Figure 14. "Mr. Ng Choy" [Wu Tingfang, later a well known foreign minister for China] was hailed as "The first Chinese gentleman admitted to the English Bar" by *The Far East* (January 1878) when he came back to Hong Kong to practice after graduating in London. Albumen print.

From the start, Black experienced difficulties in acquiring photographs, especially from China:

> *. . . and they [the Chinese photographers] will not see the necessity of sending more than a single negative of each picture, which is quite useless for the large number of prints required for each issue of the paper. European artists in China cannot supply us, their time is too valuable [expensive]* (16 May 1871, 2).

Printing the images was difficult and contributions were a permanent problem:

> *Promises of assistance were plentiful [to provide photographs and literary articles on China]; but performances were few; and as a fact no available photographs came to hand . . .* (July 1876, ii).

Indeed, illustrations covered Japan almost exclusively during the first years. Things changed in 1876, when Black moved to Shanghai; the balance reversed with China views widely prevailing. However, although native Japanese photographers had been suppliers for years, the Chinese were disappointing:

> *Chinese artists have not the slightest idea of selection. This is universally recognized; for it is a rare thing to see any views taken by them; their whole efforts being confined to the studio* (March 1877, 68).[8]

In consequence, the photographs of China published by *The Far East* were generally made by Westerners, professionals or, more rarely, amateurs.

While valuing photographs over text, and mentioning them in most of his editorial columns, Black often omitted to credit their authors. He globally acknowledged the collaboration of Baron von Stillfried in Yokohama ("our artist"), W. Saunders and L.F. Fisler in Shanghai, and some independent photographers. The future attribution of the uncaptioned views will quite certainly bring forward other names and cast a welcome light on photography of the 1870s in China.

4. THE EUROPEAN PALACES IN THE PHOTOGRAPHERS' TIME

> *What is left of the Italian-style buildings is still outstanding. A single pavilion has kept its Chinese-looking roof of purple and green glazed tiles; of the other ones, only remain standing the walls made of stone decorated with terracotta ornaments in every color* ([Devéria] 1876:2, 230).

When considering the history and impact of the European Palaces, one should keep in mind that very few people saw the site as the Jesuit builders conceived it and were able to describe it. The mystery may indeed have added to the legend. The Yuanmingyuan was the private residence of the emperor, and it is very clear that "All Pleasures [were] made for him alone."

> *This charming Place is scarce ever seen by any body but himself, his Women, and his Eunuchs. The Princes, and other chief Men of the Country, are rarely admitted any further that the Audience-Chambers. Of all the* Europeans *that are here, none ever entered this Inclosure, except the Clock-makers and Painters, whose Employments make it necessary that they should be admitted every where . . .*

wrote brother Attiret in 1743 (Attiret 1765, 87). Not even the emperor's adult children lived there, and whoever was admitted to the imperial garden was likely to be kept far from the European Palaces, in the southern area where workshops, public reception halls and drilling grounds were located.[1]

It took the disastrous Rape of the Summer Palace of 1860 to open the gates to foreigners, at first the allied armies and then residents and visitors. However, the ruins never became a favorite excursion site for the Western community or visitors in Beijing. Most of the visitors were quite happy to see the nearby imperial park of Wanshoushan as "the" Summer Palace, and to ignore the Western ruins which were so distant to their idea of China. Nevertheless, a number of photographs and descriptions make it possible to "see" the site as it was in the 1870's.[2]

What these visitors saw of the European Palaces was, of course, a far cry from the paradise so enjoyed by the Qianlong emperor. The 1860 fire had been devastating. While brick walls had remained standing, most of the graceful Chinese roofs lay in heaps of glazed tiles on the ground, and the purely Chinese structures had been obliterated. The landscape was altered too, as the carefully trimmed trees had grown wild and weeds filled ponds and basins. Flowers were gone, pave-

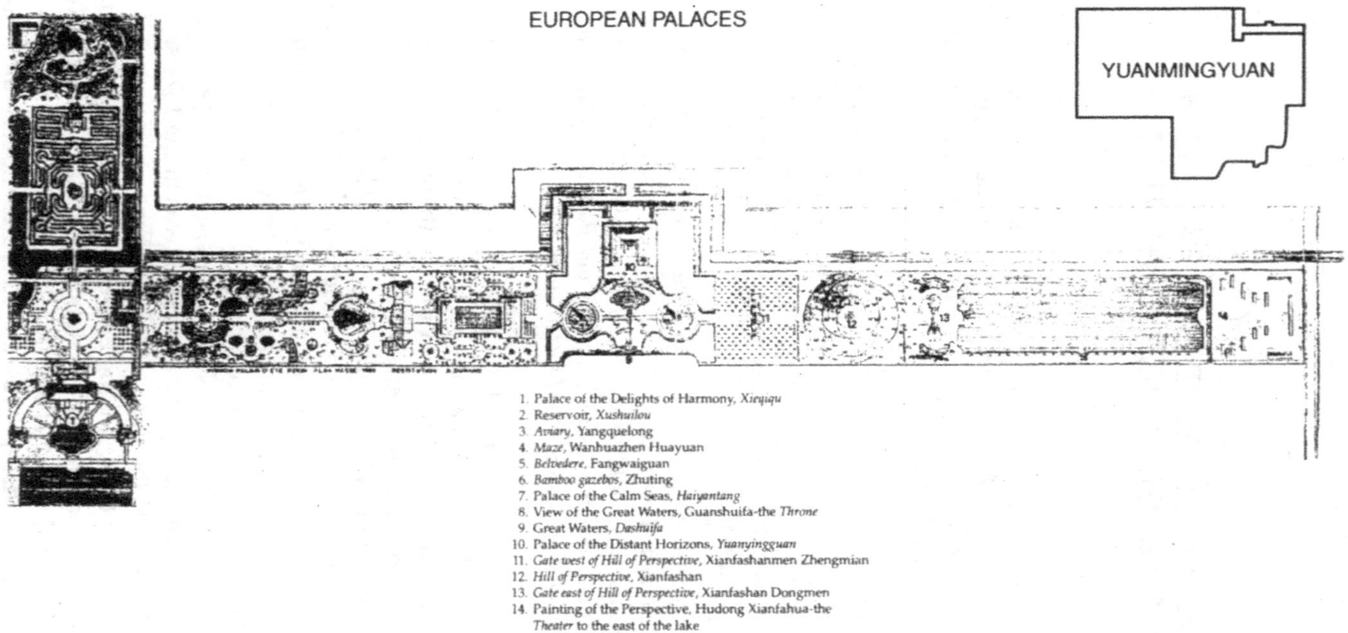

Figure 15. The European Palaces, lead on paper by A. Durand, 1985. Western and Chinese names, what is used in the text is in italics.

Figure 16. Xieqiqu, south across the lake, c. 1876, by A.T. Piry. Albumen print.

ments were bare, and many ornaments had been torn down. However, much remained to make this place unforgettable. It was, somehow, a different place, no longer a powerful emperor's dream world, but the lingering echo of a vanished pleasure palace. All in all, it had a singular attractiveness which deeply impressed its few visitors.

A Western garden, especially when designed in the French mode, provides a grand panorama enhanced by symmetry and artificiality. The plan is clear, and majesty derives from sheer size and space. A Western garden belongs to a house and provides its setting. A Chinese garden is conceived and built as a whole world unto itself, with small-scale pavilions which are its natural ornament. It is designed to lead visitors along artfully natural pathways arranged to provide ever changing and surprising views, and to guide their eyes towards the one detail which appears most perfect from a particular spot. In this respect, the European Palaces of the Yuanmingyuan may indeed have seemed more Chinese than Western.

The architects had planned twelve integrated "landscapes" in the European Garden. Each small tableau was enclosed and hidden from view by various kinds of geographical, vegetal, and architectural screens. The "landscapes" were linked together by pavements which formed the pathways to be followed by visitors. Water to be passed or crossed, rises to be climbed, screens in the form of walls, hedges or hills, all provided visual transitions linking together these "gardens within a garden" and forming them into a whole.

The Jesuits had enclosed the European Palaces area within walls and intended them to be entered from the north-east part of the Yuanmingyuan, either across a lake or through a gate. In the 1870s, however, it was easier to access the enclosure directly from the northern boundary (Rennie 1876, 36–37).

In order to retrace the steps of the emperors, the knowledgeable nineteenth century visitor (probably a man) would first have moved to the south-west end, beyond the lake which originally formed the main entrance. From there, his eye spanned the width of the Xieqiqu (Palace of the Delights of Harmony) with its two side pavilions joined to the central wing by curved galleries (Fig. 16). Deprived of its high Chinese tiled roofs, the palace appeared wide and almost reached the outside walls. On the right, the view beyond was also blocked by artificial hills covered with trees, while on the left the wall opened into a gate topped by a clock, the other main entrance (Fig. 47). Between the lake and the palace was a polylobed basin housing the fountain the emperor had enjoyed from his throne at the top of the stairs.

One could not miss its grandeur, its feeling of otherworldliness. Under the Beijing sun, the palace came alive. White marble glittered, glazed tiles sparkled, grey stone and brick in relief against the blue sky. Evergreens completed the frame. One wondered, was this palace not meant to be seen in ruins, deserted, invaded by weeds, like a mirage mirrored in water? Ernst Ohlmer, who made the comment, noted that the observer "imagine[d] standing before an enchanted fairy palace" (Ohlmer 1898, 32).

Returning to reality, the well-informed visitor would have been at pains to define the style of the unmistakably Western architecture. Baroque? Yes, certainly. Classical? In some parts, maybe. Italian? Look at these curved wings. French? Well, if you went for details . . . So, what about enjoying the lot such as it was, for all the eclectic combination of styles?

And so it went as the visitor, following in the imperial steps, reached the north terrace overlooking a courtyard with a central fountain (Fig. 19.) The small two-story building on the left (Xushuilou) seemed in good condition because it was more solid than it appeared, its windows painted on the blind wall of a reservoir feeding the fountains of the area. But across from this, only scorched earth showed where the Chinese-style aviary for exotic birds used to stand against a wall. To the north, an imposing sculpted gate (Fig. 20) cut into another wall beyond which a brick maze and the slight six-column kiosk which marked its center still made a picturesque grouping (Fig. 2.)

Yet, from the beginning of his walk to the hilly wilderness following the maze, the stroller had covered barely three hundred twenty meters. The total width of this first walled area was a mere eighty-five meters. Thus the Xieqiqu, this grandest of palaces, was really little more than a doll's house; not a place to live, only to play.

When the visitor, retracing his steps through the maze, turned into the vaulted corridor that used to form the center of the aviary, he reached another fantasy world. In the distance, majestic trees beyond a vale were striving to hide some architecture. Close by, a kiosk, or what remained of it, was reached across a bridge spanning the dry bed of the shallow river that used to wind lazily about. From there, a backward glance would have revealed that the dark corridor opened into a splendid Western gate, still intact with two niches housing fountains shaped as

Figure 17. Xieqiu, east, c. 1873, by E. Ohlmer. From wet collodion glass negative.

Figure 18. Xieqiqu, north c. 1875, ano. Albumen print.

Figure 19. The north landing of the Xieqiqu with the Xushuilou water reservoir c. 1915, by S. Black. The windows are *trompe l'oeil*.

Figure 20. Gate to the Maze c. 1873 by E. Ohlmer. From wet collodion glass negative. The men probably belong to the Customs.

Figure 21. East Gate to the Aviary in 1877 by T. Child, albumen print. See the Xushuilou through the arch.

tiered vases (Fig. 21.) This east gate of the aviary was part of the wall separating the garden into two areas, this second part a long rectangle of seven hundred seventy by sixty meters.

Moving eastward, another bridge led to the Belvedere. Hidden among trees, this small palace had, for some unknown reason, been spared by the arsonists. The purple and green tiles of its roof glittered in the sun (Fig. 22.)[3] A different fate, alas, befell the pavilions facing the Belvedere (Fig. 23,) erected in a crescent shape around their small basins; made of bamboo, they no doubt burned most cheerfully. On the ground, pieces of colored stone, glass and mother-of-pearl inlay fallen from their delicate walls were all that remained.

Further east the prospect improved. Beyond the curtain of trees stood a large construction with a very intricate fountain in its foreground. This was the Haiyantang (Palace of the Calm Seas) (Fig. 24.) The two-story structure acted as a backdrop for the fountain at the end of a large basin. In former times, the banisters of the sweeping double stairs had carried water into the basin below, spouting in gay flumes every few steps. More water had cascaded from a huge white marble shell between two rows of Daoist creatures with human bodies and animal heads standing on rocks in the pool. Each of these twelve bronze characters were meant to spurt water on the particular hour of the day they represent in the Chinese calendar, and all together at midday[4]. In 1873, however, the basin was bare and the fountain silent.

Paths skirted the palace on both sides, but the visitor was more likely to follow the emperor's sedan chair up the curved steps, across the west wing, and through

Figure 22. Belvedere c. 1873 by E. Ohlmer. From wet collodion glass negative. The damage to the emulsion apparent on the left lower corner is old.

Figure 23. Bamboo Gazebos across from the Belvedere, copperplate engraving c. 1783.

Figure 24. Haiyantang, west, c. 1873 by E. Ohlmer. From wet collodion glass negative.

a short covered stairway to the top of a huge reservoir meant to provide water for the fountains. The view from this elevation was one of great desolation. The Chinese garden to the south and west was laid to waste, while only a few charred ruins remained of the hundreds of graceful pavilions which had once graced the Yuanmingyuan.

Nevertheless, if the stroller, changing his mind, decided to circle the palace after retracing his steps, his spirit would have lifted upon seeing that part of the roof of the west wing of the Haiyantang survived and the wide facade was beautifully balanced in three parts. The surrounding garden walls were broken up into panels and their tops covered with glazed tiles. In addition, the *trompe l'oeil* north and south decoration of the reservoir of the Haiyantang, made in imitation of yet another palace, was virtually intact (Fig. 25.) The east side was a double diagonal stair leading to the terrace.

A few steps further east, the emperor had been expected to stop and discover a change in perspective. At the south end of this new area, in the 1870s a raised platform with a curved backdrop (View of the Great Waters) still awaited his throne (Fig. 26) between free-standing gates meant to allow him to make an early exit had he so wished (Fig. 44.) From the throne, Qianlong had enjoyed the play of waters in the double basin of the Dashuifa backed by marble arches crowned with bright ceramic flowers (Fig. 27.) Behind and above this, the Yuanyingguan (Palace of the Distant Horizons), with its shining white marble and veined stucco, displayed on its walls the most intricately carved decoration to be found in the European Palaces.

Proceeding east again, between two lots of trees bearing traces of earlier trimming, the visitor entered a small area closed by a massive gate, to reach the kiosk at the top of the Hill of Perspective (Fig. 35.) From there one had to choose one's way down among the crisscrossing paths in order to reach another ornate gate and a long rectangular basin. The perspective was closed in the distance by walls erected like the stage sets of a theater (Fig. 29.) At the time of their glory, they were painted to represent a small European town. Closing his eyes under the clear Beijing sky, the visitor could then imagine he was back in time, witnessing a play or concert performed for the private pleasure of the mighty Emperor of China.

Figure 25. Haiyantang, SW (reservoir), c. 1901 by A. Mumm von Schwarszenstein. *Ein Tagebuch in Bildern*, 185.

Figure 26. Throne c. 1873 by E. Ohlmer. From wet collodion glass negative.

Figure 27. Dashuifa (Great Fountain), south, with Yuanyingguan 57 meters behind, c. 1873, by E. Ohlmer. From wet collodion glass negative.

Figure 28. Gate following Hill of Perspective, westward with Hill, c. 1915, by S. Black.

Figure 29. Theater, eastward, c. 1920, by C.B. Malone.

5. THE EUROPEAN PALACES IN THE EIGHTEENTH CENTURY

In my leisure after toil, I have come for an outing . . . (Poem on the Yuanmingyuan by the Qianlong Emperor d. 1738, as quoted in Malone 1934, 63)

The European Palaces were a small enclosure at the north-eastern end of the Yuanmingyuan, the most famous Summer Palace of the Qing emperors near Haidian, twelve kilometers north-west of Beijing.

In the Western world, the word "Palace" conveys the glitter and majesty of Versailles, the grand severity of the Escurial in Madrid or the baroque wonder of the Viennese court. Nothing could be further from the design of the Yuanmingyuan. There, constructions of moderate size were part of landscapes shaped by artificial or natural relief and plantations, as well as by water, the essential element of Chinese landscape architecture.

THE GARDEN OF PERFECT BRIGHTNESS

The history of the Yuanmingyuan, or "Garden of Perfect Brightness," began with the Kangxi emperor in 1709 when Kangxi gave his son, the future Yongzhen emperor, a garden called the Yuanmingyuan near his own major summer residence of Changchunyuan. After he acceded to the throne, Yongzhen developed the garden, which the Qianlong emperor inherited in 1736 and made his favorite residence. He in turn enlarged it and beautified it during most of his reign.

For a Chinese scholar, "building" a garden was a lifelong labor of love. This was a place where creativity was at play in a refined recreation of the wonders of nature, to be shared with friends and other interested visitors. Gardens inspired poets and did much for their owner's prestige. The integration of architecture and nature was total, creating numerous small landscapes which received evocative names and were praised in poems and paintings. Covering 350 hectares, the Yuanmingyuan was also a place of refinement and seclusion. It was the emperor's private residence, accessible for the most part only to his immediate family and servants.

While in residence in the Yuanmingyuan, the emperor worked on affairs of state from 3 a.m. to 11 a.m. He then divided his time between his ladies, strolling, im-

Figure 30. Frieze on the east side of the Xieqiqu c. 1873. Detail from fig. 17.

proving his garden, reading, calligraphy, and enjoying his collections. His leisures were those of the scholar and artist he prided himself on being; he closely controlled everything produced in the imperial workshops. Usually, he had dinner between 3 and 4 p.m., and seldom went to bed after sunset.

Several gardens were grouped within the enclosed park; they are known through archives, paintings and poems. One of them was the Xiyanglou (Western Pavilions), or European Palaces. The buildings and surrounding garden were created in the middle of the eighteenth century by Jesuit court artists and scientists on orders, and under the supervision, of the Qianlong emperor. The palaces were modest in size, organized around fountains in landscapes where Chinese and Western features were used side by side and often blended.

THE EUROPEAN PALACES

The European Palaces originated from a minor incident: in 1747, Qianlong saw a fountain in a European picture.[1] The principle of spouting water being alien to China, the Emperor, intrigued, asked Brother Castiglione, a Jesuit painter at the Court, if he knew a European missionary capable of making such a fountain. The task fell on Father Benoist, an astronomer who also had some knowledge of hydraulics. Pleased with the creation, the Emperor then requested the Jesuits to build a palace as a backdrop for elaborate waterworks. The palace and side buildings

Figure 31. Yuanyingguan, south. Reconstruction, lead on paper by A. Durand, 1985.

were a combination of Western and Chinese styles and techniques. They were hidden from the Chinese garden by walls and hills, so that only the roofs were visible from a distance; as these were Chinese, nothing Western could mar the harmony of the main garden. When this first project was completed, Qianlong decided to ex-

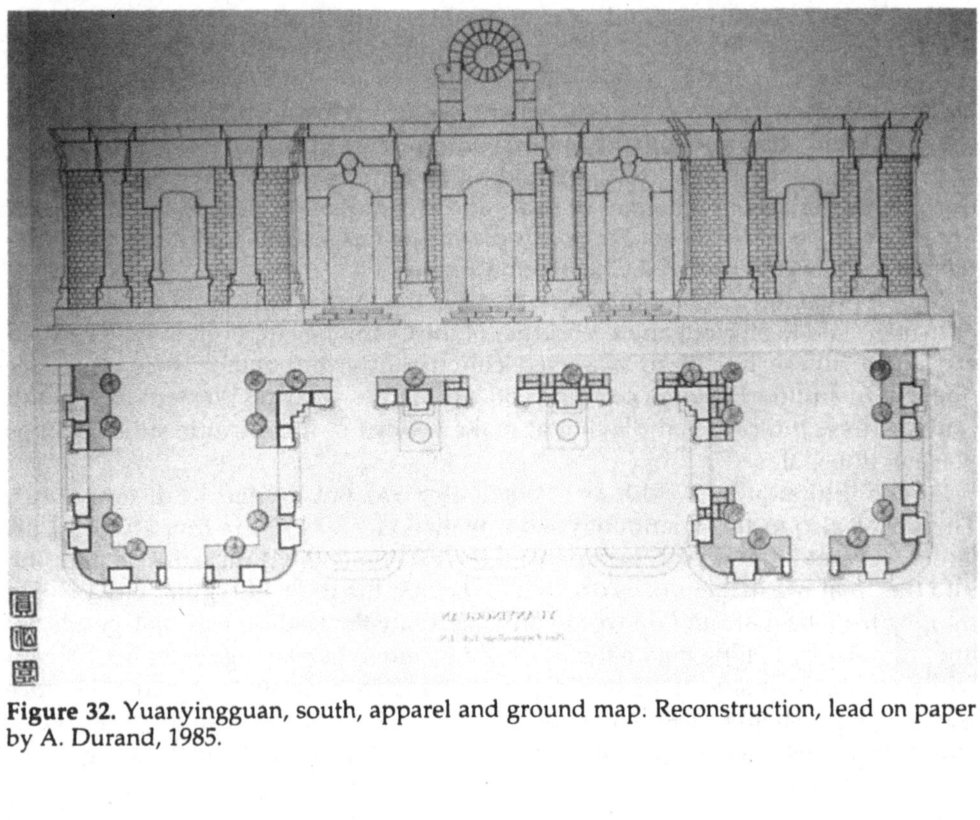

Figure 32. Yuanyingguan, south, apparel and ground map. Reconstruction, lead on paper by A. Durand, 1985.

pand upon it, until four palaces and a number of minor buildings and fountains filled a surface shaped like a reclining T, in a stunningly original world.[2]

Jesuit missionaries had been present at the court of the Emperor of China since the seventeenth century. These astronomers, mathematicians, geographers, painters or clockmakers had come to China to interest its ruler in Christianity. They hoped to achieve this by displaying their civilizations' superiority. They did not succeed in their undertaking, but their scientific and artistic achievements survived long after they were gone.

The European Palaces were never inhabited. They were mainly used to house the impressive collections of European furniture and artifacts owned by the Qianlong emperor. The gardens were a place for recreation, for strolling and admiring the fountains from various vantage points, for listening to music or enjoying the theater from a boat on the east lake.

The Jesuits' correspondence made the European Palaces known to the Western world soon after their erection. However, this fame was not accompanied by any clear knowledge. Most of what has now been established about the palaces results from recent research, in which early photographs played a significant part.

WEST MEETS EAST

The romance of distance dominated the eighteenth century, and the European Palaces of the Yuanmingyuan are, in a sense, a reverse reflection of the Chinoiseries which flourished in Europe at the same time. This interest in weaving together the traditions of east and west arose quite naturally from the fact that the Jesuit builders were themselves a synthesis of the civilizations of their native lands and of the one they had adopted. The difference of course, is, that Europe's rendition of China had to rely on hearsay, whereas in China Western designs were available first hand, distorted only by imperial interference. The European Palaces provide a precious testimony to the blending of European and Chinese traditions during this period of exchanges of ideas and techniques, of people and materials. Their flower beds displayed European plants, just as scientists in Paris, Saint Petersburg or London received Chinese specimens.

Another manifestation of this same trend is the formal portrait of a young Chinese man, said to be Hongzhan, a brother of the Qianlong emperor, in which Western and Chinese traditions are used concurrently, but retain their character (Fig. 1.)[3] In addition, several paintings of court ladies wearing Western eighteenth century dress indicate that playing at make-believe in these exotic surroundings was not unusual.

Escape into another world, or another life, was not limited to distant lands. There was also in the Yuanmingyuan a walled city where the Emperor and his ladies, several times a year, experienced the excitement and pleasure of stepping into the "real world": eunuchs dressed and acted the parts of regular city people, ranging from beggars and thieves to officials. Only the trading was real, goods being provided by Beijing merchants and sold by eunuchs playing their part.[4] Meanwhile, on the other side of the world, the young Queen Marie-Antoinette of France was playing a shepherdess in her "farm" of *Petit Trianon* in Versailles, a short distance from where had stood a famous "Porcelain Pagoda" of Chinese design.

Figure 33. North gallery of Xieqiqu from east, c. 1873, detail from fig. 17.

6. THE RAPE OF THE SUMMER PALACE AND ITS AFTERMATH

Here is what Civilization has done to Barbarity! (V. Hugo 1861)

The creation of the European Palaces in the eighteenth century accorded perfectly with the ideals of the European age of enlightenment; their destruction resulted from the powerful imperialist and expansionist European movement of the nineteenth century. No incident from any colonial war ever gave rise to as many passionate and long-lasting comments throughout the world as the Rape of the Summer Palace. This action was a far cry from the panache of the charge of San Juan Hill in Cuba in 1898, or the gallant defense of Lucknow against the Sepoy insurgents in 1857. Still, it followed the usual lines of confrontational expansion, whereby the would-be dominant civilization undertook not only to defeat a military power, but also to stamp the other culture as valueless and crush it by attacking its very symbols of hierarchy. Sometimes, however, the very act of destruction ensured that the symbols were never forgotten. Thus the legendary Summer Palace, looted and put to the torch by Franco-British forces during the last of the "opium wars" in 1860, remains a lasting memory.

INTERNATIONAL SITUATION

In the nineteenth century, East Asia as a whole was the object of Western ambitions. In China, as in Japan and Korea, the issue was not land conquest, but trade. For centuries, China had restricted the access of foreigners, enforcing drastic limitations on the circulation of Western goods and individuals. Foreign traders were only permitted to land in Canton and to remain a few weeks at specific times of the year. They were also required to use a local "compradore" as a go-between in their dealings. In the nineteenth century, the expansionist West greatly resented these obstacles to its ambitions, and, as a result, hostilities were opened by a British naval force in 1834. In 1842, the Chinese defeat in the first "opium war" led to official concessions. The Treaty of Nanjing confirmed the ceding of Hong Kong to the British crown and the opening of five "treaty" or "open" ports to international trade. At long last, Western merchants were able to reside in China and to import goods into the country. Victory after victory, treaty after treaty, foreign privileges grew and trade progressed. Faced with Western determination, China did not comply gracefully, and in 1860 events took a radical turn.

THE 1860 CHINA CAMPAIGN

The Treaty of Tianjin which opened eleven new ports to international trade, was signed in July 1858 by Chinese officials and the British and French plenipotentiary ministers, Lord Elgin and Baron Gros. One year later, it was still not ratified. In August 1859, when the European envoys tried to reach Beijing to force the hand of the Xianfeng emperor, they suffered a crushing military defeat at the Dagu forts which defended the access to Beijing at the mouth of the Beihe river.

Almost overnight, the "Chinese question" became a matter of international honor. Britain and France gathered a large expeditionary force. Having first met in Hong Kong, the armies landed on 1 August 1860 on the coast. They took the Dagu forts, then occupied Tianjin on 24 August. The Chinese, pursuing their dilatory diplomatic tactics, effectively delayed operations. On 18 September, certain their victory would not be questioned, French and British bearers of a flag of truce ventured behind enemy lines; they were taken prisoners.

The allied forces soon resumed their advance on Beijing, and passage was opened by the battle of Baliqiao on 21 September. On 5 October, in an effort to prevent the Chinese emperor from escaping to the north, the troops bypassed the capital and reached the poorly protected Summer Palace. Looting began the following day.

The Rape of the Summer Palace

First hand sources give widely differing versions of the "Rape of the Summer Palace." However, the inglorious circumstances of the destruction of the Yuanmingyuan explain to some extent the interest or disinterest of Westerners in general, including photographers.

At dawn on 6 October 1860, the troops stormed the gates of the Yuanmingyuan. The emperor had fled several days earlier, leaving only a few eunuchs in charge. Frantic looting started at once and spread rapidly to the surrounding imperial and princely estates.

The French seem to have limited their looting to the Yuanmingyuan proper because they had few horses with which to wander around. The British, well mounted, covered a much larger area and carried away heavier objects. The identity of the looters is still discussed on occasion. Without question, both armies were involved. The coolies hired in the south by the armies and the local population also had a share in the take.[1] After three days, on 9 October, the French and British armies retired towards Beijing, which surrendered on the 13th. The Summer Palace was handed back to the official care of the imperial guards, but sporadic looting went on.

It has always been accepted that the British were solely responsible for the dev-

Figure 34. Arch of west gallery of the Xieqiqu showing cracks caused by fire, c. 1873. Detail from Fig. 17.

astating fire which ravaged the Summer Palace, the French having distanced themselves from this symbolic act of destruction. By 8 October, the first prisoners taken on 18 September had been returned to the allied armies then camped near the Yuanmingyuan. They were soon followed by the coffins of those who had not survived captivity. Faced with the evidence of the sufferings inflicted, and despite the surrender of Beijing, the British extraordinary ambassador, Lord Elgin, decided to retaliate against the person of the emperor, judged responsible for the outrage. The punishment was the destruction by fire of the Yuanmingyuan. This order was broadly interpreted. The torching of all the imperial estates in the looted area took place on 17 and 18 October. Approximately one hundred forty square kilometers were set afire by British troops, two thousand men being employed in this destruction for two days. The Qianlong emperor's dream world disappeared in flames. So did the great quantity of remaining artistic and cultural treasures which had escaped the looters and for which the Yuanmingyuan had been so famous.

Chinese architecture, which is constructed with wooden columns bearing the heavy weight of the roof and devoid of masonry walls, is extremely vulnerable to fire. Eyewitness accounts of the burning of the Summer Palace describe the systematic, at times painstaking, progress of the arsonists, the buildings ablaze and collapsing in heaps, the fire spreading to trees, etc. Military discipline ensured that the work was thorough. There are no photographs of the disaster itself, or of the

Figure 35. Pavilion on Hill of Perspective c. 1875, ano. Albumen print.

ruins immediately afterward, but many were made in the area during the succeeding years, long showing desolate ruins and charred tree trunks.

Western Comments

The Rape of the Summer Palace became known in Europe by the end of December 1860, and was an instant sensation. Public reactions ranged from reserved to negative, especially concerning the fire. In January 1861, the House of Lords, gathered in London to vote the nation's thanks to the army, had a stormy meeting (*The Times*, 15 February 1861). A controversy about who had done what immediately arose; evidently, the recent alliance between France and Britain, after centuries of belligerence, did not extend to trust. The bulk of the French press had relied at first on the official report and, refuting the British newspapers' version, denied that

Figure 36. Haiyantang, west. Line engraving by Therond in *Le Tour du Monde* (1864:2, 111.)

looting had occurred at all.[2] Then, a first account of the "*Sac du Palais d'été*" was published in Paris on 28 December, fully contradicting General Cousin de Montauban's report from China, and the truth could be denied no longer.[3] The argument soon took a patriotic turn. France lamented the burning (by the British), while the British press piously denounced the looting, done solely, some claimed in the face of evidence to the contrary, by the French army. Meanwhile, the Rape of the Summer Palace had become folklore.[4]

Overall, the judgment put on the deed was negative. The great French poet Victor Hugo claimed in an open letter, "We call ourselves civilized, and them barbarians; here is what Civilization has done to Barbarity!"[5] Even those who believed the destruction had been necessary to force China to compromise, deplored the loss of so much beauty.

Yet, despite all the controversy, Cousin de Montauban, the French general-in-chief in China, flatly denied that there had been any looting by his army. He stated that the soldiers had "received with all regularity [. . .] [the] few objects [. . .] [they had] spontaneously" offered to the French Emperor and Empress. He stuck to his version in March of 1874, offering the British press another occasion to ridicule what had remained the official French position. It did so with relish, and published fresh eyewitness accounts of the event.[6]

The topic remained current for a long time. In Beijing, Western residents or visitors openly decried the destruction of the palaces and collections. If, in 1876, a

French diplomat who had lived in Beijing for several years wrote about "the strength we were constrained to use in order to attempt to force China out of a systematic isolation violating all divine and human laws" ([Devéria] 1876:2, 307), he seems to have limited his approval to the sole concept of the campaign.

THE LEGEND

The Yuanmingyuan was never rebuilt, although this was seriously considered for the Chinese gardens and their wooden architecture, ruined beyond recognition by the fire. During the years 1871–73, work was begun on the Chinese section. The Dowager Empress Cixi intended to retire there since the young Tongzhi emperor, her son, had reached his majority and her regency was over. Tongzhi's untimely death put an end to the matter. Thereafter, what construction materials could be salvaged were reclaimed by Cixi for the construction of the Yiheyuan (Park of Peace and Harmony in Old Age), the new Summer Palace begun in 1886. The Yiheyuan incorporated the Wanshoushan (Hill of Myriad Ages), another imperial garden damaged in 1860. This is the Summer Palace in Beijing so familiar to modern visitors.

Constructed of brick and stone, the European Palaces had withstood the great fire much better than their wooden Chinese counterparts. Since there was no question of including anything Western in the New Summer Palace, the ruins were left undisturbed, consigned to oblivion, their walls still standing years later in the Beijing countryside. Only recently have some conservation measures been taken, first with a careful rearrangement of architectural remains before the Cultural Revolution and, since 1984, with a massive effort at restoring the site which has paid little attention to historical or architectural accuracy and has altered landscape and ruins beyond recognition (Barmé 142–158).

Especially in China, however, legends survive long after the physical reality has vanished. Towards the end of the nineteenth century, the story of a beautiful lady from Akesu (Xinjiang) became attached to the European Palaces. It was said that she had been taken prisoner when her husband was killed fighting the Chinese armies and that the Qianlong emperor then took her into his household against her wishes. As her body exhaled a delicate fragrance, she was known as Xiangfei, the perfumed concubine. She lived in the European Palaces, and the Belvedere was converted into a mosque to allow her to practice her religion. But despite Qianlong's efforts, she never forgot her previous life and threatened to kill the emperor if he ever approached her. In order to protect her son, the Dowager empress, mother of Qianlong, took advantage of his absence to order Xiangfei to commit suicide. It has now been clearly demonstrated that the story is only a legend, but certain paintings of a Chinese lady in Western dress are still said to be portraits of her. Too lovely to be soon forgotten, Xiangfei will doubtless remain linked forever to the memory of the European Palaces.[7]

For indeed, as time passed, the tiny enclosure of the European Palaces—one-fiftieth of the total area of the Yuanmingyuan—became the most famous part of the garden, simply because it was better preserved than the rest. The Xiyanglou recall

Figure 37. Xieqiqu from the west wall ca. 1915, by E. von Perckhammer. On the left behind the ruined Xieqiqu are visible the Xushuilou (reservoir), the partition wall with the maze, and the rectangular pavilion behind the maze. *Peking*, 188.

older and glorious times for China; for many, they are the essence of the whole Yuanmingyuan. Paradoxically, the architecture conceived by Western minds has become a symbol of Chinese loss from Western brutality. Perhaps this is because today only imagination allows the visitor to "see," in the few remaining stones, the world of dream-like fantasy created by exiled Jesuits working for God's—and the Emperor of China's—glory.

THE EUROPEAN PALACES, 1860–1940: FROM RUINS TO RUBBLE

The flamboyant sacking of the European Palaces was a major historical event; their subsequent disintegration was quiet, although ultimately far more lethal. Photographs record the stunning extent of the damage inflicted through the years by neglect and pilfering. Nowadays, very little remains of the European Palaces as they appeared to the 1870s photographers. Somehow, the fate of the Yuanmingyuan reflected that of the Chinese nation itself: scorched by the Franco-British invasion in 1860, tortured by the 1900 Boxer Rebellion and its aftermath, looted by the warlords who confiscated the newborn Republic of 1911, and, finally, crushed by the misery accompanying the Japanese occupation. Unlike the nation, the garden never had a chance to recover.

As stated above, the buildings and garden were never restored, or even maintained beyond the most basic fencing. One of the contributions of photography to the study of the site of the European Palaces is the recording of its relentless decay. In addition, the older images testify to the damaging effect of the 1860 fire. As early as 1873, most of the scorched marble lintels had disintegrated, giving the openings

Figure 38. Belvedere c. 1915, by E. von Perckhammer. *Atlantis* (February 1931:90).

of the palaces a strange vaulted look. Heated to high temperature during its manufacturing process, ceramic withstands fire well: thus the inlaid decoration was mostly intact, while the tiled roofs lay in large heaps on the ground. Not a door or window survived the blaze. The inside walls were gutted, bare brick showing where sculpted wooden panels had once hidden them. A few constructions escaped torching, as they contained no wood (Gate to Aviary, kiosk on Hill of Perspective). Other places were spared at random by the arsonists (Belvedere, kiosk in Maze). As later images show, however, nothing survived the passage of time.

The process of destruction took many years, to be mostly completed by 1940. Intriguingly, the images also reveal the structure beneath the surface ornaments of this make-believe world where every effort was made to have even blind facades appear like welcoming halls. In some cases where the nature of the construction material was unclear, its condition provided the answer: stucco coating tends to crumble, but marble and stone break, the first more cleanly than the second. There is also, most importantly, the proof that eighty years of pilfering had been far more destructive than the blaze and were ultimately responsible for bringing the European Palaces to oblivion. Although created as playthings, the Jesuit walls were, in fact, very well built to last so long under such conditions.

A major clue to dating the photographs between several states of the same view, is the progressive elimination of the decorative elements. Marble and stone slabs are more easily removed than inlaid ceramic, and generally reveal a brick core. This relative dating, of one image against another, is done print by print. Photographic technique is not a factor: there was only one major improvement over the period, the change from the wet collodion process to silver gelatine, which, moreover, is unclear on the prints. But why try to date the images with precision, apart from a certain taste for tidiness? First, dating the views allows us to determine which of the different states shown of a given place is closer to the original. Secondly, since the 150-odd photographs identified before 1925 cover half a century, it would be difficult to study them without using some form of chronology or/and identification system. But there is a third and more far-reaching reason. Dating the photographs is a key to authorship, and sheds light on the photographers themselves. There is no doubt that in most cases this advances the history of photography in China more than the study of the Yuanmingyuan; yet, on occasion this exercise has led to the discovery of other lost images of the European Palaces. It also provides some insight into why these photographs of ruined palaces were ever taken; that is, what they meant for people such as the young German Customs officer Ernst Ohlmer in 1873.

The surviving photographs supply a chronology of the destruction of the palaces. Between 1873 and 1877, the top ornaments disappeared in both the Dashuifa and the nearby Yuanyingguan.[8] Among other milestones, we notice that the marble balustrades decorating the stairs of the Xieqiqu were pushed to the ground before 1876; the top level of the palace then started crumbling, even before the garden was once again totally closed to visitors about 1886. The next photograph, about 1901, is a stunning vision of destruction (by the Boxers, by allied foreign troops and/or by scavengers?), the palace reduced to a pile of rubble with only one major wall still intact, interior columns and arches standing almost ob-

Figure 39. East Gate to the Aviary c. 1915 by S. Black.

scenely in the open (Mumm ca. 1902, 182). Already, the well-named Palace of the Delights of Harmony (Xieqiqu) was only a memory (see Fig. 37.)

For other areas, the worst was yet to come. The link with the local political situation is clear: while the unrest of the Boxer Rebellion had opened the door to destruction by all parties, the following years of relative quiet showed few visible changes in what was still imperial property. The onset of the revolution which spelled the end of the Qing dynasty brought new upheavals; graffiti was noticeable by 1910, while numbers painted on slabs and other elements of marble around 1915 suggested a plan for imminent dismemberment.[9] Still, it was not until the severe troubles of the Warlord period in the 1920s that the site became a large local quarry for bricks. Systematically, the marble and terracotta ornaments were torn away to allow access to the core of the walls and to this material, essential to construction in north China. There is a very telling image of what the photographer called the "Peacock Cage" (the gate to the Aviary) as it was being dismantled almost overnight in 1924 (Malone 1934, 146).

Concurrently, from 1910 on, even before the fall of the dynasty, the ground was progressively leveled for cultivation, and trees disappeared from the enclosure. The little nooks and crannies, hillocks and vales, so carefully designed to please and surprise the eye, were wiped out to make way for fields. The ever smaller piles of construction material were pushed closer together in shrinking islands marking the site of the former European "follies." A stunning photograph made about 1940 during the Japanese occupation shows the once lush and hilly garden, now flat and bare, except for a deep trench where the partition wall had formerly stood (Fig. 41.) Everything that could be of any use had been carried off while the vegetation was vanishing, creating a lunar landscape stretching unbroken to the distant Western Hills.

Figure 40. Haiyantang, west, c. 1923, by S. D. Gamble.

Figure 41. Haiyantang with the Western Hills in the distance, c. 1940, by H. Morrison.

PART II: PHOTOGRAPHERS OF THE EUROPEAN PALACES

Throughout the years, scarcity was the major obstacle in the search for photographs of the site: one hundred and fifty views are very little to cover, over half a century, four main palaces, a number of small buildings, and many interesting vistas. What is uncommon is not known. (As a consequence, for the first few years, whenever writing in search of photographs or visiting a collection, the researcher found it necessary to provide an image as a reference.) This is how the study expanded far beyond the palaces themselves, and how interest switched from the photographs of the European Palaces to the men who made them. At method level, it was also natural to look at all relevant material on an individual basis; conducting the same type of study for all could not have done justice to any one of them.

Based on all known images, the photographers of the European Palaces neatly fall into two large groups. They represent either early photography in Imperial China (1873–78) or modern technique in a new Republic (1911–1925). The distinction goes further than time and state of the palaces: most of the material related to each of the later photographers was found gathered in a single repository, while the early material had been wildly scattered over a number of countries. Consequently, the research had to be conducted in much greater depth for the nineteenth century photographers, since detailed biographical and photographic data had to be collected from different sources before reaching any kind of conclusion. In contrast, for the second group, there was usually no need to go beyond the photographs of the European Palaces. The connection between the two very different groups of men and photography came with an album produced in 1901, the halfway mark of the study. In addition, beyond their views of the palaces, the photographers were all attractive as research subjects. In fact, each deserves to be the object of a dissertation on his own.

THE MARITIME CUSTOMS MEN IN THE 1870S

7. THE IMPERIAL CHINESE MARITIME CUSTOMS

For in those days all white men on the coast held together and sank their separatist tendencies (King 1924, 18).

Three sets of photographs essential for the study of the European Palaces were made between 1873 and 1877. And their authors, Thomas Child, Ernst Ohlmer and Théophile Piry had more in common than the subject matter of their photographs: all three were in Beijing in the service of the Imperial Chinese "Maritime" Customs. This fact is not incidental, for it meant that they knew more about China than most of their contemporaries, in addition to sharing living quarters and offices. They probably also influenced each other in their decision to record the European Palaces for posterity, when so many Westerners were avoiding the site,

They came from England, Germany and France, young men who ended up spending between twenty and forty-five years in China. That the three were from nations sometimes antagonistic was unimportant for the powerful corporate culture of the Customs Service overwhelmed differences in nationality and language, dominating both their professional and private lives. There was more in common between Ohlmer and Piry, a German and a Frenchman six years after the German armies had inflicted on France one of the worst defeats in its history, than, say, between British merchants and missionaries in Shanghai. Still, it was a strange twist of history, that this Chinese civil service, created by Westerners to serve their own trading interests, became, thanks to the competence of its foreign staff, a pillar of stability and modernization for a country suffering from troubles which owed much to foreign interference.

The Customs Service, often labeled "maritime" (*Haiguan*) to distinguish it from the native customs (*Changguan*), was set up in July 1854 to facilitate international trade. From the start, it was run by Western men; it was confirmed by treaties in 1858 and 1860. Contrary to other taxes, the Customs income was paid to the central treasury, hence its importance to the government. Over the years, it came to guarantee loans raised abroad, as well as payment of the successive war indemnities inflicted on China.

In 1863, a twenty-eight-year old Irishman, Robert Hart (1835–1911), became the second Inspector General of the Maritime Customs. Two years later, the Inspectorate was officially moved from Shanghai to Beijing. Ten years after its creation, the organization of the Service, such as it would grow, was set. The Inspector General answered directly to the newly created *Zongli Yamen*, the Grand Council committee in charge of foreign affairs. He was assisted by local commissioners in charge of the ports, who supervised assistants of various ranks. Control was exercised by "The Indoor Staff [. . .] where the Assistants attended to the levy of duty on goods examined by members of the Outdoor Staff. The latter also boarded and searched the vessels plying to and from the port" (Williams 1969, 16). (A third service, Marine, maintained the harbors and lights, while the Coast service assured surveillance and assistance at sea.[1])

The history of the Customs is closely linked to the personal history of Robert Hart. Arriving in China at nineteen in 1854 as an interpreter in the British Consular Service, he was appointed to the Customs in 1859. Together with his knowledge of China and its language, the quality of his advice regarding international matters gained him the trust of the Chinese ministers. He was soon appointed head of the Service, a position he held for forty-four years.

Hart was a remarkable organizer. However, it has been written with good reason that "The key to [the Customs Service's] success was that it avoided encroaching upon vested interests of the Ch'ing (Qing) bureaucratic behemoth. Rather, it lived off the new growth of foreign trade" (Hart 1991, 202). And the Inspector General's attitude is summed up in the phrase he constantly reiterated to his staff: "Remember that you are a Chinese and not a foreign official." Although a Westerner living a Western life in China and never tempted to forget his origins, Hart was first and foremost a civil servant devoted to the government he served. The fact that this loyalty to China never hurt his credibility with Western governments is a credit to his acute sense of diplomacy.

For the selection of his foreign personnel, Hart went far beyond mere appreciation of capability. Quotas of nationalities were instituted, in relation to the respective countries' share of trade with China. Qualified men from the consular or diplomatic bodies were attracted to the Customs by the higher pay. In addition, the staff and Hart's numerous contacts were encouraged to present suitable candidates. Study of the Chinese language, strongly advised, soon became a condition for promotion. As stated in Employment Agreements entered into by Indoor Service employees in 1903:

> *(1) I must perform all duties assigned to me; (2) I must study the Chinese language, literature, manners and customs [. . .] (5) I may be dismissed for [. . .] failure to pass an examination in Chinese in three years* (Williams 1969, 15).[2]

Such requirements went far beyond those of any other firm or service in China, where most foreigners never learnt Chinese. In spite, or perhaps because of this, the average length of career for Indoor personnel was thirty years, a very long time in any respect.

Ohlmer and Piry were recruited for the Service directly in China (the applications of young men from Europe were usually processed through the London office of the Customs.) Candidates, aged nineteen to twenty-three, were assessed on their education. In those pre-typewriter days, a neat and legible handwriting was essential, as was fast arithmetic. In addition, Hart stated, "I want them to be young and bright—I mean likely to learn [. . .] how to live in China, how to get on with messmates, how to talk to the public" (Hart 1975, 167). To this end, the examination included lunch in a private club to check the applicant's social manners.

Like most foreigners, the newcomer received a Chinese name, the transcription of his Western name for Chinese use. He was assigned to one of the major ports as a clerk; thereafter, he moved every two or three years. New ports were opened to foreign trade along the coast or on the Yangzi river and experienced assistants were put in charge when the low level of traffic did not justify the presence of a commissioner. They had full authority in the running of their office, answering directly to the Inspector General.

Hart was in command of everything, including appointments at all levels. Personal preferences were rarely considered. A man could find himself moving from the tropics to the freezing north on very short notice. Housing being provided, newcomers often took over the furniture and servants of their predecessors. Except for a few ports like Shanghai, Tianjin or Lappa (Macao) where Western suppliers were sufficient, purchases were mail ordered from the nearest large port or from Europe (the United States had a parcel service only in later years). Every seven years, the Indoor service people were entitled to two years leave of absence with half-pay, usually spent in the West. Some took advantage of this time to resume studies in law or other useful subjects, while others were given special missions abroad.

Promotions depended on the man's professional qualities, his knowledge of Chinese and other languages, his tact and diplomacy, but also on his personal re-

Figure 42. Group at the Inspectorate General of the Customs in Beijing, 14 November 1881. Albumen print by A.T. Piry. From left, sitting are Piry, Hillier, Hart, Farago and Bredon. Standing are Spinney, Brazier and Montgomery.

lationship with Hart. Undoubtedly, a stint in Beijing, at the Inspectorate General, furthered the career of competent men. Piry, a mere third Assistant B, was put in charge of a newly opened port after only three years in the Service—half of which had been spent in Beijing. Extra professional skills also counted; it was said in the Service that a musician, or a man whose wife played an instrument or had a pretty voice, had a higher chance of being called to Beijing by Hart, a great music lover.

In fact, none of the three photographers owed his appointment to the Inspectorate General to his artistic accomplishments, although Piry claimed a pleasant singing voice. Child was hired for his technical skills, while Piry and Ohlmer entered the Indoor Service through a "back door." Piry was recruited in 1874 on probation, and Ohlmer was granted a rare move from the Outdoor to the Indoor Service. Still, they enjoyed successful careers. Both men confirm the appeal of the Customs to young men richer in ambition than in wealth or connections: in the end, competence was what really mattered.

The foreign supervisors' duties went far beyond strict Customs concerns, in large part because of the Inspector General's special relationship with the Chinese government. Many enjoyed the variety:

> *There is a good deal to the fact that you may be called upon at any moment to drop blue-pencil and manifests and become an Inspector of Forts, a Naval Commander, an Embassy* Attaché, a *Postmaster-General, a drill sergeant or a secret agent . . .* (Williams 1969, 18)

Piry was for a time professor at the Tongwenguan in Beijing. He concluded his career as Postmaster General. Ohlmer acted as a mediator during negotiations between the Chinese and German governments. Other commissioners took charge of the Chinese contributions to international exhibitions, escorted embassies abroad, or pondered the selection of ships for the Chinese navy.

In 1874, thirteen men lived in the Inspectorate General compound in Beijing. Seven were actually working in the office, and four studied Chinese. The doctor was attached to the London Missionary Society and taught at the Tongwenguan, and Thomas Child was "gas engineer." They were of five different nationalities. Like Beijing society, this was a very small and almost exclusively male world.

Life was not very exciting in mid-1870s Beijing for a young Customs man. Office hours were ten to four, six days a week, but, even if the working day was more intense than in the legations, there was time to spare. The conditions were the same as those at the nearby legations whose inmates were met with at every opportunity. The daily life described by the diplomat W.H. Wilkinson, in Beijing about 1880, was similar to Ohlmer's or Piry's. They shared a same type of domestic setup in mess, amusements and neighbors.

*

* *

> *I wish we could get some fellows [. . .] who would make a name for themselves and for the Service by literary and scientific work out here*

wrote Hart in 1874 (Hart 1975, 167). He succeeded in this also. The Customs Service sponsored publications by its men on a variety of subjects related to China. These efforts counted for promotion.

The intellectual involvement of Customs officers in the study of their host country was real: in 1901, seventeen percent of the members of the North China Branch of the Royal Asiatic Society in Shanghai belonged to the Service. The Customs press in Shanghai published numerous literary and technical translations from or into Chinese done by Customs people. This was how Piry published the French translation of a Chinese novel and a Mandarin-English-French dictionary.[3] A few of the Customs periodical publications, including the medical and meteorological reports, became established institutions in their own right.

This erudite tradition was carried on after Hart's departure in 1907. H.B. Morse or S. Wright's studies on China and the Customs remain important reference works. L.C. Arlington, author of *In Search of Old Peking*, and C.A.S. Williams (*Outlines of Chinese symbolism and art motives*) also left informative accounts of their time in China. Other men had artistic bents: Ernst Ohlmer, Ivor Daae and Alfred Hippisley assembled important ceramic collections.[4] Paul-Georg von Möllendorf was charged with acquiring a collection of Korean art for the Peabody Museum of Salem, Mass.[5] The Customs also counted in its ranks the future writers J.O.P. Bland and Putnam Weale, as well as Prosper Giquel, soon to be a Chinese general and founder-director of the Fuzhou arsenal; all were able to use their Customs experience and contacts to foster second and brilliant careers.

Such was the professional, social and cultural environment in which the nineteenth century photographs of the European Palaces were produced.

8. THOMAS CHILD
The Photographer of Old Beijing

The photographs taken by Thomas Child provide the main reference point for nineteenth century photography of the European Palaces, as well as for imperial architecture of Beijing in general. He is also the only "professional" studied here. His almost unbroken residency in the capital between 1870 and 1889 allowed him to create, in his spare time, the earliest photographic inventory of the area.

The geographical coherence of his images, the extensive circulation they enjoyed for a long time, and the physical characteristics identifying them, open the way toward compiling a corpus of Child's work in China, to which this chapter could be seen as an introduction.

THOMAS CHILD, 1841–1898

Thomas Child is the only photographer of the European Palaces to have been studied by historians of early photography in China.[1] He was born in 1841 in Madeley (in Shropshire, England), the son of an engineer. He taught technical subjects in London and was also, at least by 1869, an amateur photographer. In May 1870, he was hired by the Customs as engineer in charge of the gas works in the Inspectorate General in Beijing, where his wife and three children joined him in 1874. In 1889, the family returned to England and settled in Bromley, a south London suburb. Child met an accidental death in 1898. Although his family kept "*Chang-an-Tang*" (sic.), his house in Bromley, until 1960, there are no traces of his photographs among his descendants' papers.

Now considered a professional photographer, Child did indeed sell his work. However, this was never his official occupation, and he really pursued two simultaneous careers while in China.

THOMAS CHILD, PHOTOGRAPHER

Child stands out in the field of early photography of China. He did not practice studio-type photography, but concentrated on monumental architecture. He appears, in fact, to be responsible for creating the type of photography thereafter associated with Beijing; contrary to Shanghai or Hong Kong, where typical scenes of daily life were always enjoyed, Beijing photography long dealt primarily with monuments.

Child built an inventory of views of the extended Beijing area. Although his work has not yet been fully inventoried, no serious study on Beijing architecture or nineteenth century photography in China can ignore him. He recorded a great number of buildings and monuments no longer extant and, in many cases, his were the earliest photographic records. Sometimes—as with the gate to the Aviary and the Princes Porch in the European Palaces (Child Nos. 203 and 206)—his were the *only* views taken before defacement or destruction.

His work also provides a clear time reference. His portfolio was built between 1870 and 1889, and many images were dated by year. Thus, the state of numerous sites at a specific time was preserved, and serves to date other early photographs of Beijing.

Child's approach to his subject was straightforward. If the better known views by John Thomson (1871) are similar on occasion, they are very different in nature. Monuments acted for Thomson as supports for his observations of the Chinese people, while for Child they were an end in themselves. Significantly, his large portfolio did not extend to photographs of private homes.

The technique of wet collodion he used was delicate, and those who mastered it were usually good photographers. Ohlmer and Piry's plates are of the same excellent quality as Child's. However, the latter had an exceptional command of outdoor photography during the very cold Beijing winters, when chemicals altered and washing water froze on the plates. He even skated on the ice at the Wanshoushan, creating spectacular views from the lake.

Child seems to have started his Beijing photographic work with portraits, of which few examples are known. He left also a few scenes of daily life. They were shot in private, or show the people of Beijing (his servants?) during outings which presumably had photographic purposes. A rare scene bearing the manuscript comment, "Wheel Barrow loaded with 1 ton 5 cwt of coal brought from Tung Chow (Tongzhou), 14 miles in less than 4 hours by 3 men and a donkey," shows the authors of the feat in a courtyard, the human ones smiling into the camera in one of the most authentic and attractive scenes of Chinese life produced at that time (Fig. 43.)[2]

Identifying Child's Work

Child's images of China were widely collected. Many prints can be found, scattered in a number of collections. His style, both in photography and in printing, is recognizable. The photographs are often dated and/or signed, numbered and captioned, while Child's range of action was limited, both geographically and in time. Moreover, in 1877, the artist published a list of his commercial work.

Nevertheless, the identification and recording of his work are not so easy. The information was muddled by Child's very success, as quantities of copyprints were made in the photographer's own time and later. The later prints often distort

Figure 43. No. 174, c. 1875. Albumen print with signed handwritten caption by T. Child.

his characteristic features of size, tone and inscriptions; it is also common to find different "original" inscriptions on several prints of the same image. Moreover, the samples are widely scattered across the world, rendering the crucial comparison of print to print physically impossible. Thus, the process of recording is a task totally out of proportion to the volume of his portfolio, which probably numbers no more than four to five hundred views.

It should be noted that copyprinting in itself is not proof of fraud. Child's wet collodion plates were exposed to sunlight for printing; multiple repeats having faded his first negative, he had to create another one. Thus he probably copyprinted his own photographs, creating images similar in color and size to the originals, with only a small loss of definition and depth. On the other hand, with the most active forgers, accidents to the older prints reappear from copy to copy; the image is cropped to hide repeated damage, and its quality visibly deteriorates.

As shown from good prints,[3] Child's own production is uniform in tone (a rich brown) and size (about 25 x 20 cm). Later copies tend to be larger, darker and lacking in depth. In addition, Child's images bear a number of distinctive inscriptions, in the form of signature, date and title.

The most common inscription is the signature, which normally appears in black, a simple manuscript "T. Child", or "Tho$_{s}$. Child" in letters which seem clumsy because they were carved in reverse on the emulsion side of the plate; some plates

Figure 44. West Princes Porch (north), d. 1877. Line engraving from T. Child's photograph No. 206 in Bonnetain, *L'Extrême-Orient* (1888, 347).

were also signed several times. A rare exuberant variation, about 1875, included an eight-shaped flourish under the name. This is also the time when dates first appeared inscribed below the signature, sometimes together with the caption "Peking."[4] The script is very sharp on the originals, but becomes fuzzy or disappears on successive copies.

In addition, many prints show a number and title. In China, captions on photographs became common in the 1880s, and were often added to older images. The usual form was a black box at the bottom with white lettering. As with everything else, Child was distinctive: his titles appear directly on the image, in clear, well-balanced capital letters. On occasion, the caption was either replaced or supplemented by a slip of white paper bearing a number, a title, and a few lines of description.[5] In contrast to the signature, the caption was always located in the lower left hand corner, and thus sometimes overwrote earlier inscriptions.[6] Its presence is an important clue to the sequence of production of the prints.

The last mark, more rarely found, is the photographer's oval stamp, reading, "THOS. CHILD, PEKING". Its two forms include a purple ink stamp on the back of the print with the number pencilled in the center, and a dry stamp in the same shape at the edge of the print. The latter seems to be authentic, but the former is found on copyprints produced long after Child was gone and could actually identify a forgery.

Child's intent of creating a commercial series is confirmed by the number and title, which also pre-suppose the existence of a list. Indeed, Child started advertising such a list in the Shanghai journal *The Far East* in July 1877, seven years after he had arrived in Beijing.[7] It is loosely arranged by subject, from the Summer Palace area, the city walls, the Imperial City, the Temple of Heaven, the Great Wall and Ming Tombs, back to the Western Hills near the Summer Palace, together with a few mixed views.

An item by item comparison of the list with the numbered prints (caption or slip) reveals that, while wording may vary between list and prints, the gist is the same. It also appears that although only one hundred forty-eight numbers out of one hundred ninety-two were used on the original list, in the following years the photographer filled most gaps left in the sequence of numbers. He also added numbers up to 208, including the European Palaces (196–208).[8]

Unfortunately, matching titles from the list with images can only be done through numbered copies, which leaves out a number of images, as well as gaps in the list. Although he used his photographic plates sparingly, Child made similar shots, sometimes years apart. There is no problem with "No 150. Ancient Arch Nankou Pass" (Juyongguan, in a spur of the Great Wall), for which a number of fully captioned copies exist. But many images, including most of the earliest collected, bear only an undated signature; there is no certainty that an uncaptioned image is really the one listed in 1877. A case in point is No. 141, "The Great Wall," for which two versions are found, a rare view dated 1875, and a more common one from 1877.[9] It is clear that negatives were replaced under the same number and title as need arose.

Captions also appear at random on images, apparently unconnected with the diverse combinations of signature, "Peking" and/or date, and thereby confirming that inscriptions could be added or altered at any time.[10] To summarize, based on the prints studied and their context, it appears that Child's original inscriptions developed over time from (i) no signature, date or title; to (ii) signed, undated; (iii) signed, dated; and, last, (iv) signed, dated and titled. In addition, most prints are not originals, but copyprints.

Captioning seems to have begun sometime during the mid-1880s, when Child could have entitled the whole collection he was then offering for sale. The process would have started with a slip of paper pasted under the print between 1880 and 1887. The photographer soon added the number and title on the image, and that caption ultimately replaced the slip. And in fact, most late copyprints bear at least remnants of the original titles, indicating that they were copied from material produced after Child had captioned his plates. This also explains why some earlier, never captioned images, are rarely seen: they were not found on that late market.

Thomas Child and *The Far East*

The importance of Child's work in the early history of photography of China is demonstrated by its rapid and sizeable publication by various authors, as well as by *The Far East*, then published in Shanghai.

Advertisements.

THE FAR EAST,

Illustrations in Vol. 3,

continued:—

Yucca Gloriosa, in the Public Garden, Shanghai.
Monseigueur Verroles.
Mouth of the Woosung Creek.
Chungking, Szechuen.
A Szechuen Family.
Mandarin Garden Retreat.
H. I. H. Higashi Fushimi no Miya.
Cemetery, Dai Toku Ji, Nagasaki.
The Tablet of "Yu."
Water Gate at Kwenshan.
Inside the City of Kwenshan.
Carrying a Maternal Uncle—Chinese woodcut of a Chinese Drawing.
From Chungking, Upper Yangtsze.
General le Gendre.
Bridge at Sungkiang.
Group of Aborigines, and Hut Formosa.
The Foaming Cascade, Amoy Province.
The Temple Lam-poo-too-Mian, near Amoy.
A Quarrel.
Fort Zelandia, Formosa.
The Residence of Chu Fu-tsze, near Kinkiang.
Sledges for Winter Travelling on the Frozen Rivers, North-China.
Pekingese Car.
Pekingese Lady.
A Chinese Nun.
An-ching, on the River Yangtsze.
Bridge and Creek at Hongkew.

VIEWS OF PEKING AND ITS VICINITY.

TAKEN BY.

MR. THOMAS. CHILD.

VIEWS IN "WAN SHOU SHAN" (part of the Summer Palace).

1—Front General View S. side.
2—View from Lake ,,
3—Temple of Universal fragrance.
4— do do do End view.
5—Six-sided pagoda.
6—Small bridge.
7—Dell and Temple.
8—N. W. View.
9—N. E. ,,
10—Porcelain Pagoda.
11—Bridge and Arches.
12—Bronze Temple.
13—Stone Junk.
14—Pagoda Bridge.
15—17 Arch Marble Bridge.
16—Camel back do
17—Bronze Lions.
18— ,, Cow.
19—Bridge and ruins.

VIEWS IN "YU CHUAN SHAN"—" (Jade spring hill)" also part of the Summer Palace, 2 miles from Wan Shou Shan.

30—Water Dragon Temple and Pagoda.
31— ,, ,, ,,
32—Marble Pagoda.
33— ,, ,, Base of
34— ,, Sculpture S.E.
35— ,, ,, S.W.
36—Porcelain Pagoda.
37—Temple and ,,
38— ,, Porcelain Pagoda.
39—"Yu chuan" The Jade spring.
40—Cave of the Gods.
51—View in the grounds.

FROM THE PEKING OBSERVATORY.

46—Front from below.
47—View from City wall.
48—Bronze Armillary sphere.
49—Bronze Astrolobe.
50— ,, Globe S.E.
51— ,, ,, ,,
52— ,, N.E.
53—General View of all at top.
54—Bronze Armillary sphere, top.

FROM THE CITY WALL.

56—Examination Hall No. 1.
57— do No. 2, Summer.
58—Head of Grand Canal N.E. corner of city wall.
59—Ha-ta-men (Great Street from City gate).
60—Chen-men (Front gate.)
61— ,, (house on top of)
62—Ta-ching men "Emperor's gate"
63—Nan Saug "Portuguese Cathedral."

IN IMPERIAL CITY.

71—Coal Hill, S.E. view.
72—S.W. View of Coal Hill, moat, and corner of forbidden city.
73—Ta Kow tien, the worship in the temple is the same as in the temple of Heaven.
75—Marble Bridge.
76 N.E. from do Palace grounds.
77 N. ,, ,,
86 Yellow temple—Lama temple.
87 Incense burner.
88 Marble monument, front.
89 ,, ,, side.
90 ,, ,, pilan.
91 ,, ,, details of
94 Mongol encampment.
95 ,, ,, small.

IN TEMPLE OF HEAVEN.

96 Covered altar.
97 ,, ,,
98 ,, ,, View looking north.
99 Altar of Heaven.
100 ,, ,, Details.
101 ,, ,, and Pilau.
102 Gate of South temple.
103 Sacrificial furnace.
104 Well and slaughter house.
111 Great Bell Temple.
116 Pali chuang pagoda.
117 ,, ,, and Temple.
118 ,, front of ,,
119 White pines.
121 Confucian Temple.
123 Entrance with stone drum.
126 Hall of Classics.
127 Marble Pond.
128 Pilau.
129 Tablet house.
131 In Hunting Park. } Shung yun
132 Fish pond in ,, } ,,
133 Pagoda in ,, } Shung shan
136 Ju Yuen Sue (Temple).

NANKOW PASS ON WAY TO GREAT WALL.

141 Great Wall.
142 ,, with gate.
143 View in Pass.
144 ,, Great Wall in the Pass.
145 Great Wall; top of Pass (Pata ling).
150 Ancient Arch (Che Yuan quan).
146 ,, Mongol Wall Watch tower north of Peking.
147 Ancient Mongol wall Tablet by Emperor Kinlung.
148 Ancient Mongol Wall and Barbican.
198 Ancient Yen remains of Walls S.W. of Peking.
153 Marble Pilau.

MING TOMBS.

154 Avenue of Stone animals.
155 ,, ,, Men.
156 Entrance to Yung lo's tomb.
157 Yung lo Hall.
158 ,, tomb.
159 Tang shan.
160 Hot spring.
161 View in grounds.
162 ,, ,, Island Post.
163 ,, ,,
166 Senping Tai (Summer residence of foreigners of Peking).
167 Chang Aim Sai with cemetery.
168 Shi Ching shan.
171 Peking Cart.
172 Mule litter.
173 Sledge on ice.
174 Barrow with 1 Ton 5 cwt of Coals brought 14 miles in 4 hours with 3 men and 1 donkey.
175 House of little Ease.
276 Ta foah Sai.
178 Nestorian tablet.
179 Chinese group.
180 Audience 1873.
181 Student's Quarters. British Legation.
182 Gate in French Legation with Chinese.
183 Gate in French Legation.
184 Great Lama and attendant.
185 Butcher's shop.
186 Lu Kuo Chow No. 1
187 ,, ,, ,, 2
188 ,, from top.
189 ,, looking N.
190 Cloudy Waters Cavern Entrance.
191 ,, Gorge and steps.
192 ,, Gorge.

VIEW IN ENGLISH CEMETERY PEKING.

Any of the above views—size 10 ins × 8 ins may be obtained, Price 50 cents each, through the

FAR EAST AGENCY.

5, Honan Road, Shanghai.

Figure 45. Inside cover of *The Far East* (July 1877) showing the list of photographs offered for sale in Shanghai by T. Child through the offices of the journal.

Geographically isolated as he was in Beijing, Child must have found in this attractive journal an excellent opportunity to advertise his work. Between July 1877 and November 1878, he gave them five photographs.[11] This was a period of intense photographic activity for him: the majority of his plates are dated between 1875 and 1878. In the journal, the quality is only fair; the images were copyprinted to half the size. Child may have provided original prints which were copied in Shanghai both for the journal and direct sale.

In fact, *The Far East* was probably more important to Child as an advertising and distributing venue than for its limited readership. In September 1876, the journal had announced the creation in Shanghai of "The Far East Art Agency," for the sale of photographs "and other Works of Art." "In a short time extensive and interesting Portfolios and Albums of Pictures of Interesting Localities and Characters in China and Japan will be on View." Child's list fit in well with this program.

In January 1878, *The Far East* had agents in the major open ports of China and Japan, as well as in New York and in London, and, not surprisingly, Child was the agent for Beijing.

CHILD'S LEGACY

Judging from the quantity of prints that survived and the comments they received, the nineteenth century public liked photographs of East Asia. No collected series, however, could compare in influence with the illustrations published in books and magazines. Here again, Child is a major reference. His images were used for direct representation of architecture, as well as for documentary support of historical events, some of them occurring long after he had left China.

The photographer was English, yet his views of Beijing enjoyed their greatest success in France. The most influential work was probably *Peking* by the French Roman Catholic Bishop of Beijing, Alphonse Favier. Favier made wide use of Child's work, both as photoengravings and as woodblock engravings.[12] The plates are possibly the best known source for photographs of the European Palaces to this date and were copied in a number of subsequent works.[13]

But already in 1887, *L'Extrême-Orient*, a book by Paul Bonnetain "illustrated with numerous sketches from nature" had presented Child's views of Beijing and the Yuanmingyuan. The engravings copy their model accurately, although in one amusing instance Arabian camels were introduced to fill in a gap in a bird's eye view of the Qianmen (Child No. 60). Bonnetain (1858–1893) was a journalist with the French newspaper *Le Figaro*. He visited East Asia in 1882, seven years before Child's departure. His scattering of so many of Child's prints (37 in the 1888 edition) throughout his description of China, was homage in itself and proved that the Englishman was a major source. Indeed, Child's photographs can be found at random in a number of travel or topical books published at the turn of the century.

Still on the topic of Child's eminence, a sizeable series of postcards of Beijing from the early 1900s shows a square stamp inscribed, "Th. C. Pékin." The views are later than Child, and the style more modern. Apparently changed from "collection Th. Culty," the presentation seems to have been an attempt to cash on Child's name.

A surprising legacy of Child's also derives from the common practice of engravers recomposing images. The London journal *The Graphic* presented in January 1895 (57), "From a photograph by Mr. Thomas Child, of Pekin," a full page image of the Emperor of China, riding in a closed sledge drawn on the ice by eight running men in front of interested onlookers, with skaters in the background. The basic ingredients for this composition were Child's No. 78, "View in Imperial City. Peking," and a sledge made in Europe for the Emperor (*The Graphic* 1894, 660). The two photographs were combined, a few actors added, and the improbable whole presented to readers as an authentic representation of the Son of Heaven's winter pastime.

Along the same line, in December 1894, the same journal had shown "Archery drill by Chinese soldiers in the streets of Pekin, from a sketch by Thomas Child, of Pekin." Although Child did photograph (but not sketch) the archer, the roofs have a Japanese slant, while the city walls and Arabian camels are purely North African. This image of China, revised by the common denominator of exoticism, is an interesting illustration of the dangers of indoor reconstruction.

In fact, the very neutrality of Child's work, in which the subject stands isolated, central to the image, made it an ideal support for photographic reconstructions.

Figure 46. The Emperor's Sledge, based on a photograph of the Beihai lake in the Imperial City by T. Child (No. 76). *The Graphic* (1894:660.)

Because the photographer did not convey any personal interpretation of China, it would be difficult indeed to define his personality from his commercial work. Instead, he provided a framework for any real or imaginary conception of China. This is probably why he remains current today, while the typical scenes so popular with other early photographers of China have become mostly symbols of a time when John Chinaman was no more than an object of curiosity, if not of contempt, to the "enlightened" Westerner.

9. ERNST OHLMER
Sailor, Photographer, Customs Officer and Porcelain Collector

Although laid to waste and overgrown by vegetation, these buildings still had an enchanting effect in the mid-seventies [. . .]. The observer [. . .] [could] not suppress a sense of deep melancholy reflecting that in this enlightened age it had still been possible to pointlessly destroy that splendor! (E. Ohlmer 1898, 30–32, tr. A.W. Mixius)

Ernst Ohlmer was a young German who had been established in China for several years when he came to Beijing in 1872 and discovered the enchantment of the European Palaces. An amateur photographer, he was the first to record them. Whether in terms of quantity, selection, homogeneity or quality of the images, his 1873 series provides an exceptional source for the site.

ERNST OHLMER (1847–1927)

Ohlmer was born in 1847 in Betheln, near Hildesheim in the kingdom of Hanover (Germany). The eldest son of an innkeeper, he studied languages before signing on with the merchant navy. The family history (a project started at his instigation after his retirement) states that he passed Cape Horn, a milestone for a sailor of old. He was shipwrecked off the Chinese coast, and "it was clutching a board that he was pushed toward shore by the waves" (K. Ohlmer, 33). He began his life in this new country as a professional photographer.[1] Soon changing professions again, "after he had learned the local language," he joined the Outdoor Service of the Imperial Maritime Customs on 1 May 1868. His first appointment was to Amoy (Xiamen in Fujian).

From 1868 to 1914, Ohlmer's life was shaped by the Customs Service, in which he enjoyed a successful career. In August 1872, he was transferred from the Outdoor to the Indoor Service. He remained in the Beijing office from 1872 to 1880 as private secretary to Hart, and then as an auditor. In the words of Hart (1975, 671), he was "a very reliable workman, and both neat, willing and painstaking."

He married in 1885 and, until 1898, alternated standard port positions and postings in Beijing. Personal archives are missing, but a few sources help to recreate the setting of his daily life.[2] Frank Spinney, an American commissioner, followed him in Canton in 1887, taking over his house. Spinney's wife Annie's letters to her family go into detail about the house and furniture, servants and colleagues, and life in general in the Western settlement of Shamian island on the Pearl River (Letters dated 4, 6 and 10 July 1887, Spinney papers, PEM). The vegetable garden grew produce. Milk and fruit were local, but many other staples were ordered from Hong Kong, or even from Europe. Because the water was too dirty in Canton, laundry was done in Hong Kong, only a few hours away by steamer. Many necessities came the same way, whether it was ice for cooling or a Chinese tailor. The letters include the sketch of a dress deemed "light" and suitable for tropical life, complete with bustle over corset. But maintaining Western standards was not always hardship; later, a photograph showed Louise Ohlmer driving her own carriage in Beijing, the only one in the capital in 1895.[3]

In 1897, because it lacked territorial holdings in East Asia in spite of its sizeable economic interests in the region, Germany used the excuse of the murder of two missionaries to land troops at Qingdao (Shandong). In March 1898, it was granted a ninety-nine-year lease on the area (Jiaozhou) and its waters. Although still Chinese, the territory was effectively ruled by Germany which set up a free trade zone in Qingdao. Following negotiations in Berlin during which Ohlmer represented Hart, the jurisdiction of the Chinese Maritime Customs over goods circulating beyond the Qingdao territory was recognized. In this delicate context, it was necessary that the Customs commissioner be a German national.

As a result, in March 1898, Ohlmer was put in charge of the Qingdao Customs. While he had been appointed for political reasons, there was no doubting his loyalty to the Service. Hart noted in 1905 that "the Tsingtau (Qingdao) Germans don't want" Ohlmer (Hart 1875:2, 1485). Obviously, he was not considered sufficiently devoted to German interests. He nevertheless remained in office. As the Customs Service's rule of transferring people regularly was ignored when appropriate, Ohlmer retired in 1914 after sixteen years in Qingdao. He went back to Hildesheim, but his house in Qingdao in 1899–1900 still bears a plaque in his memory.

OHLMER, PHOTOGRAPHER OF THE EUROPEAN PALACES

When this research started in 1987, Ohlmer's name and most of his photographs of the European Palaces were already known. His last unpublished images came to light soon afterwards. But several years followed before more information on Ohlmer and his photographic work could be unearthed.

The Photographs

The first step had been a slim volume in Chinese entirely devoted to the subject: *Ruins of the European Palaces of the Yuanmingyuan*, published in Shanghai in 1933 by Teng Gu. It included fourteen views of the European Palaces, and one map of the site dated "Nov. 1873." The comment on pages 1–3 stated that the photographs had been taken by Ernst Ohlmer "Commissioner of the Customs in Tianjin," and the plates turned over to the art historian Ernst Boerschmann by Ohlmer's widow. (Nevertheless, it was easy to see that one of the views was Child's (pl. 15, Child No. 206), and the last one a modern view of the Dashuifa. In addition, Ohlmer was never posted in Tianjin.)

Then, in July 1987, from London came a photographic album described in Christie's catalogue as, "Yuan-Ming-Yuan, Summer Palace, Peking [. . .] majority architectural views." A pencil note indicated that the album had previously been in the collection of Sir Robert Hart (which could not be confirmed.)

Teng Gu had linked the negatives to Ernst Boerschmann. This was verified: in 1988, the grandson of the architect/art historian was located in Berlin and found to have the twelve published negatives, which also made the trip to Paris. They were wet collodion on thick glass, about 20.5 x 26 cm, in good condition although one was broken in the middle as already visible in the book. The set was simply inscribed "Yuen Ming Yuen 1931," without any other documentation.

The album purchased in London was concertina-bound in blue silk and the prints followed the order of the garden, with one exception. The first photograph was Teng Gu's small map of the European Palaces dated "Nov. 1873." Then came fifteen views of the palaces, full page and slightly trimmed, followed by other subjects.

The images were hand-tinted in places in a clumsy way and sometimes erroneously. If not accurately placed, all colors were seen on the site, and from one view to the next, details were consistent. Was this the work of a Westerner unused to painting albumen prints? Interestingly, the only plates colored were the European Palaces, although the Chinese architecture of the following pages would have been even more colorful.

This set constitutes the oldest known photographic record of the European Palaces. While the faded album lacks clarity, this is fully made up for by the negative plates. Their focus is outstanding, and the virtually unlimited potential for printing enlargement permits a thorough examination of details.

Altogether, the views are more than mere reflection of a lost imperial architecture. They also show the violence of the 1860 fire. Damage is blatant, stone and marble severely degraded. Yet, in a more positive note, the photographs reveal numerous details of the building material, the shape of the sculptures, the roofs, etc.

In 1987 details from the album were photographed and enlarged, then the negatives became available and were printed. It became clear that the kiosk of the Maze was made of bricks (base), wood (columns), ceramic (pediments and roof tiles), stone and marble (pediments inlays, crown moldings). Experiments with time exposures highlighted details. They revealed, for example, that the seemingly wrought metal openwork grate filling the arch of the gate to the Maze was actually sculpted wood, and that the decorative circle crowning the Yuanyingguan was made of ceramic (Fig. 27, 48.)

Documenting Ohlmer became a priority, in the belief that he could lead to the discovery of new photographs. It was easy to establish that the man had indeed belonged to the Customs, then to outline his career and to locate his place of birth.[4] An intriguing guidebook was traced.[5] It was discovered that a major attraction of

Figure 47. Clock gate near Xieqiqu, c. 1875, ano. Albumen print.

the Roemer-Pelizaeus Museum in Hildesheim is the Ohlmer collection of Chinese porcelain; the guidebook had been published in 1898 for the opening of the new Chinese gallery.

Ohlmer left no children. He belonged to a large extended family long established in the area (the family tree goes back to 1570) but, because he had left Germany as a teenager and lived in Hildesheim only from 1914 to 1927, his cousins know little about his life. Louise von Hanneken, his wife, survived him. On her side of the family, Ohlmer's nieces were not even aware that he had ever made photographs. In the end, despite the assistance so generously provided, local and family sources were disappointing. Ohlmer's reputation as a collector had cast a veil over his photographic activities.

While there was enough material attesting to Ohlmer's authorship of the series of photographs of the European Palaces, a twist appeared. The guidebook of 1898 credited all the photographs to Ohlmer, but plate III, a south-west view of the Xieqiqu (Fig. 16), was made by his friend Théophile Piry a short time later: thus the crediting was not fully reliable. And finally, two new sets of photographs of the European Palaces from the same period came to light a few weeks apart in 1994. There were two prints in Durham, England, and four in the small town of Uslar, not far from Hildesheim; in the last collection was also found an original of the Xieqiqu by Piry.[6]

Do the two sets belong together, how did they reach Uslar and Durham, and, more importantly, what is their connection (or lack of) with Child, Piry, and/or Ohlmer?[7] Three prints in Uslar—two of them European Palaces—show by transparency Ohlmer's name in block letters in ink on the back. But was he named as

Figure 48. Dashuifa and Yuanyingguan c. 1873 by E. Ohlmer. Detail from fig. 27.

the photographer, the owner, and/or the supplier?[8] The inscriptions seem to raise more questions that they answer.

Even for the album, things are not so clear. However, Customs sources state that the young Ohlmer was in Beijing from August 1872 to April 1880. His guidebook clearly dates the photographs from 1873, and so does the map found with them.[9] In addition, the album ends with four groups of Westerners. One print is also found in the Hart papers in Belfast, where it is inscribed, "Wan shou shan March 7th 1874." For that date, Hart noted in his diary, "Hessie [Mrs. Hart] & all the world have gone to *Wan shou shan* to a pic-nic given by the *Nan-yuan* people."[10]

There is no doubt that Ohlmer's views of the Xieqiqu predate Child's (1877–78) and Piry's.[11] Moreover, Piry, who arrived in Beijing in December 1875, does not appear on any of the photographs.[12]

The Photographer

The research showed that in general, Ohlmer's photographic work is quite forgotten. Presumably, most of his self-acknowledged production is lost among the thousands of anonymous prints which form the bulk of collections of early photographs of China. However, one large album was found in Hamburg; it had been dedicated on 23 March 1872 to one C. Blumberger, by "A-li-wen"—Ohlmer's Chinese name.[13]

This is an outstanding volume, bound in leather with stylized dragons at the corners. Most pages present large and beautifully printed landscapes and buildings which are mounted at the corners like the Ohlmer Yuanmingyuan album.[14] They show Amoy (Xiamen in Fujian) and the nearby town of Zhangzhou. There follows one page on Formosa (Taiwan), a few views of the Shanghai area, and then a series of much smaller street and genre scenes done in the usual Shanghai style. An amusing personal touch appears with a view of the Shanghai Customs House, with a pencilled arrow pointing to the "Pay office!" All pages except the scenes bear the same elegant type of caption; that is, large Chinese characters and two different transcripts (based on Mandarin and Fujian dialect, the latter in German gothic handscript).

In contrast to the large landscapes, the small Taiwan images and scenes of daily life appear to be copyprints. The scenes were clearly shot by a studio and designed to illustrate "native" Shanghai life. With their poor printing and movement blurs, they look like rejects. The question is, are they Ohlmer's, mementoes of his time in a studio, or were they collected by Blumberger to be added to the album? They are only captioned in German, and are not identified as to place. They also are part of a larger series traced in other albums.[15]

THE COLLECTOR OF CHINESE PORCELAIN

As established above, Ernst Ohlmer is remembered largely for his Chinese porcelain collection. He helped establish a Chinese Art department in the Roemer Museum in Hildesheim. His collecting activities started early and were strengthened by those of two other Germans in China, the diplomat Max von Brandt and the Chinese general Constantin von Hanneken. Each had his own area of specialization: von Brandt collected the Blue and White porcelain, von Hanneken the monochromes, and Ohlmer the polychromes.

The Three Collectors

Max von Brandt (1835–1920) spent most of his diplomatic career in East Asia. He came with a Prussian mission in 1860, and became consul in Yokohama in 1862. When he was appointed minister to Beijing in 1874, negotiations over the opening of a legation had been going on for several years, to finally succeed in 1875. In his memoirs, von Brandt acknowledged Ohlmer's assistance for preparing plans and estimates for the building, translating them into Chinese and adapting them together with the local contractor (Brandt 1901:3, 29). The two men became close; with so few Germans in Beijing, the usual class barriers faded. Brandt retired in 1893. He left a number of books on East Asia and a reputation as a learned collector. Nothing from his collections or archives acquired by two Berlin museums seems to have survived World War II.[16]

Constantin von Hanneken (1854–1925), the third important collector, was the son of a Prussian general and a military engineer. After a short stint in the German army, he went to China in 1879 as a military instructor for Li Hongzhang, the powerful viceroy of the northern province of Zhili (modern Hebei) and an influential advocate of Western progress in China. He soon became an instructor for the navy with the Chinese rank of general. He was on board the transport *Kowshing* when the vessel was sunk at the onset of the Sino-Japanese war in 1894; he had to swim for his life, as had his brother-in-law thirty years earlier (Ohlmer had married Hanneken's sister.) Hanneken married in Tianjin the daughter of Gustav Detring, a Customs commissioner close to Li Hongzhang. The only one of the three collectors to maintain real ties with China, he died in Tianjin in 1925.

Ohlmer, Brandt and Hanneken all had official positions in China and this certainly facilitated their collecting activities. Ohlmer assembled most of his collection in Beijing between 1872 and 1880 before, as he put it, "only Croesus could afford this luxury," the prices being pushed up by the arrival on the market of the Western antique dealers (Ohlmer 1898, 27).

The Roemer Museum

During his years abroad, Ohlmer maintained close ties with his native land of Hildesheim. In 1878, the city museum (not yet named after its president, Senator Roemer), asked him to assist in the purchase of a collection of Chinese and Japanese artifacts (porcelain, stoneware, lacquer, bronze, enamels, ivory, etc.), "old and superior quality pieces" (Roemer to Ohlmer, 9 February 1880, cited in Wiesner 1981, 9).[17]

Ohlmer would ultimately contribute to the collection both as a donor and agent for the purchase of artifacts. With the years, his involvement grew, from the 1880 offer of items from his collection for display to a gift in 1881 to lending his porcelain, painting, textile and furniture collection to the new Chinese Department in 1898. The loan included one hundred forty items he had collected and one hundred fifty Blue and White porcelains purchased from von Brandt; von Hanneken also lent his collection to the museum. The guidebook published for the opening was one of the first studies on Chinese porcelain written in German.

The three collections illustrate what could be acquired in Beijing during the 1870s, when the impoverished nobility was slowly selling off its collections. Ohlmer noted later:

> *There are still in the princes' and high-ranking civil servants' palaces, many treasures which come to light now and then and are sold to the moneylenders or to the antique dealers, especially at New Year, when needs are pressing because of insufficient income and salaries [which have been suffered] for many years . . .* (Ohlmer 1898, 26).

Purchased from Chinese collectors, these objects differ from the great collections gathered outside China. They belong to the Ming and, predominantly, the Qing periods.[18]

Ernst Ohlmer and the Yuanmingyuan

There is no doubt that his love of porcelain is what led Ohlmer to the European Palaces. Chapter IV of the guidebook entitled, "Chinese use of porcelain and stoneware in vases and statues, as well as in architectural decoration" was, after two vague paragraphs on vases and statues, devoted entirely to architectural ceramics.

A short description of the palaces of the Forbidden City in Beijing served as an introduction to the European Palaces, "what is probably the most ravishing of all." As an Auditor, Ohlmer first had to estimate the cost of the construction of the European Palaces,[19] but then he went on to evoke the enchanting mood of the place. The profusion of shapes and colors of the "Fairy Palaces" were recalled in a lyrical style in utter contrast to the rather dry study of the history and manufacture of Chinese porcelain which made up the rest of the volume:

> *The decoration [. . .] had been given all the colors and nuances of the rainbow [. . .]. You see the rich and lively colors of the ornamentation, saturated by the deep blue Peking sky, kaleidoscopically changing according to the position of the viewer and of the sun, standing out boldly against the white marble background of the building, and at the same time being like a ghostly mirage reflected in the lake facing it [. . .] The observer cannot help feeling like in a fairy-tale from "A Thousand and One Nights"* (E. Ohlmer 1898, 32. tr. A.W. Mixius).

It seems, in short, that Ohlmer saw in the ruins a splendid museum of polychrome ceramics, and there is no doubt that his fifteen plates are the best iconographical source on the subject. He carefully preserved twelve negatives (the three missing ones were presumably lost or destroyed before 1932), and ultimately left them to Ernst Boerschmann. Yet what was the connection between these two men, when did they meet, and why did the negatives go to the art historian? Boerschmann's diaries are currently being studied in England, and may eventually open a new phase in the history of Ernst Ohlmer's photographs of the European Palaces.[20]

10. A. THÉOPHILE PIRY
Forty-Five Years in China Through a Camera Lens

One of the foreigners living in Pakhoi [. . .] has a genius for amateur photography (*NCH* 2 September 1879, 232).

The Frenchman Théophile Piry is the third of the Chinese Maritime Customs men. He was an "amateur" in the true sense, one who knows and values passionately an art which is not his profession. Of the photographers of the Yuanmingyuan, he is the one who recorded China and the European Palaces for the longest time; his photographic activities can be documented over more than thirty-six years, from his first exposure of the European Palaces to the last one, in a link between early and modern photography. Himself very much a man of the nineteenth century, he developed in China a twentieth century postal system. He also left behind an important photographic legacy centered on his family, in which his views of the European Palaces seem almost accidental. Piry held important acknowledged positions in both the Chinese Customs and Postal Services,[1] but his work as a photographer has been largely ignored.

Piry's name first came to the author's notice in 1987, attached to a photograph of the Yuanmingyuan; however, he was nowhere recorded as a photographer and his connection with China was not clear. But a few months later, his name appeared again in a bibliography leading to an article published in 1901 by Mr. Théophile Piry "of the Chinese Maritime Customs." Data on the Customs previously collected to document Ohlmer immediately confirmed that Piry had indeed belonged to the Service, and that he had been posted to Beijing in 1876–77. Yet no mention whatsoever was made of his photography.

Then, in 1989, a book published in 1904 came to the researcher's attention. It printed photographs by "Piry" of the 1900 Siege of Beijing, the first clear indication that this man had indeed been a photographer. A few months later, his photographic collection was traced to his grandson, Charles Blackburn. His hundreds of small glass negatives included new images of the European Palaces, while letters provided a solid personal context.[2]

In retrospect, Piry appears as a case study of how an in-depth research starting from a single photograph can proceed to a satisfactory conclusion. Honesty also compels the author to recognize that this was the only step-by-step research which directly brought to light new images of the European Palaces.

A. THÉOPHILE PIRY (1851–1918)

The major private source of documentation on Théophile Piry are three letterbooks (bound volumes in which correspondence was copied) kept by Charles Blackburn together with a few other family papers.[3] In addition, the archives of the services Piry had belonged to document his career. It would appear that his photographic activities were closely related to his life in China. He enjoyed a privileged position in several ports in succession as well as in Beijing.

Théophile Piry was born in 1851 to a working-class family in the trading port of Nantes. He arrived in China in 1870; his elder brother, Pierre, had been in the Chinese Maritime Customs since 1857. From 1871 to 1874, Piry worked at the French-founded arsenal of Fuzhou (Fujian), as either a professor or a secretary.[4] In 1874, when the running of the arsenal was turned over to the Chinese authorities, Piry joined the Chinese Maritime Customs Service in Shanghai as fourth Assistant B "on probation" (a rare restriction). He was rapidly confirmed in his rank and received his first promotion a year later.

In November 1875, he was called to the Inspectorate General of Beijing where he remained for fifteen months. He then received the charge of Pakhoi in Guangdong (Beihai, now in Guangxi), a port between Hong Kong and the French colony of Tongking (in Vietnam) being opened to international trade at that time.

Piry's letters from Pakhoi reveal a very lonely young man (in 1877, there were only five Westerners in Pakhoi), but one fully aware of the opportunities offered and determined to succeed. He dutifully reported to Hart the problems encountered and the solutions he had applied; there was indeed room for initiative in such a posting. In his plentiful spare time, Piry also undertook to translate a Chinese novel and started resuming Latin studies; this is how one could enhance one's career prospects in the Customs—by demonstrating one's command of the Chinese language and one's culture (Piry to Pierre, 1880). His leisure activities included sailing, shooting and, as will be seen later, photography.

Piry returned to France for the first time in thirteen years in March 1883, after a second posting in Beijing as Assistant Chinese Secretary (interpreter). His future was safe. He was back in China in 1885 with a young bride, his cousin Isabelle Jeffray.

His appointment to the Korean port of Pusan (then Fusan) was proof of Hart's trust. Korea was at that time a sensitive area for the Chinese Customs. A nominal vassal of China, the country had long been coveted by Japan; it would actually become a Japanese protectorate after the Sino-Japanese war of 1895. The Korean Customs Service had been created in 1883 outside of Hart's control to remove trade restrictions between Japan and Korea. In 1885, the Chinese Customs took over in a statement of China's suzerainty. In consequence, the Customs representatives had some political weight.

Most of Korea's international trade was with Japan and went through Pusan. Piry settled in the Japanese concession, on a hill overlooking the harbor. His letters reflect the absorption of a young father very much involved with his little family. His wife and children were already the exclusive focus of his concern, as they would remain for the rest of his life, and the words reveal nothing about Korea or its inhabitants. They are, however, a mine of information for studies of Western domestic life in an isolated East Asian port. Most of the family's supplies came from abroad, and Piry wrote the orders.

His letterbooks provide lists of preserves available at Mustard and Co. in Shanghai, from sardines to camembert to *foie gras*. All orders were shipped through Nagasaki in Japan, from whence fresh staples came by overnight steamer, including the weekly supply of French bread from the baker Salvéry. The publisher of the *Rising Sun* newspaper in Nagasaki provided stationery, but books were ordered from Kelly & Walsh in Shanghai. Some items were ordered directly from Europe. In September 1887, Isabelle's father, a widower, was sent a long list of clothing to purchase at the *Bon Marché* department store in Paris. (A sign of the times, the list included a "dressy" embroidered dress for the young Alphonse, a sturdy little boy, and corsets for Jeanne, size one year to eighteen months.) Photography was not mentioned in this correspondence, but a few album pages of Pusan remain.

The Pirys were in Korea from May 1886 to September 1888. They subsequently moved several times, to be in Lappa (Macao) ten years later. Piry was offered the directorship of the Korean Customs, but lost the position by refusing to commit himself without guarantees (Collin du Plancy to Piry, 3 February 1898). Remaining with the Chinese Customs, he was again posted to Beijing, and this was in several ways a turning point.

For several weeks after he arrived in Beijing, Piry's professional life, his private life and his photography were closely linked to world news. This was May of 1900. After years of increasing demands and extortion of privileges by the Foreign Powers, a powerful anti-Christian movement had developed in China. The "Boxer Rebellion" started with general unrest in the provinces and rapidly reached Beijing where, after considerable destruction of missionary property, foreigners were physically attacked. On 9 June, the Customs families were moved in haste into the legations compounds; four days later, the Inspectorate General was set afire. The actual Siege of the Legations started on 20 June with the murders of the German minister and his Japanese colleague. Foreigners and Chinese converts were besieged in the capital. This very difficult situation lasted until 14 August, and during these "fifty-five days of Peking," when the worse was always possible and often probable, Piry photographed the besieged. One of the images shows "The Volunteers of the Customs." Piry appears on the side wearing a bush hat, having just set the camera; the child with a gun in the first row is his son "Théo" (Fig. 49.)

During the Siege, the family and the Customs personnel stayed at the British legation. The eldest boy, Alphonse, was at school in France, which left Piry with his wife, their children Jeanne, Isabelle, Théophile and Nalka, the youngest at four, and the children's governess.[5]

Immediately after the end of the siege, which Piry celebrated by taking his camera to the Temple of Heaven, the Customs evacuated the married men and their families, while the Beijing office was reopening in temporary accommodations. In October 1901, returning at the end of a special leave, Piry was put in charge of the Postal Service. He kept the position until his death, and it rapidly became very important.

Théophile Piry took over an infant service closely dependent on the Customs and made it into an independent and modern organization. Since the field was new to him and to his staff, he made up for deficiencies by learning from postal ser-

Figure 49. "The Volunteers of the Customs" in 1900, by A.T. Piry. From a silver gelatin glass plate negative. Piry is standing on the right with a bush hat; the child in the middle front row is his son Théo.

vices from other countries, especially France.[6] Administrative methods were borrowed from the Customs and for a long time so was the personnel. Piry managed to preserve in his Service the international character which had been so successful with the Customs; however, he was certainly more influenced by the French government than Hart ever was by London.

Just as the Customs Service did with the sea and river ports, the Postal Service undertook to link the towns and cities of China. There was, however, a major difference in scale. While in 1907 there were forty-one open ports, the postal offices and agencies grew from 176 in 1901, to 7,763 by 1913. At all levels, the percentage of Chinese employees was considerably higher than in the Customs because times also were changing. In 1911, the Postal Service employed 120 foreign managers from twelve countries, 462 Chinese managers and 14,462 Chinese postal workers ("Mélanges" 1911, 575).

Keeping the Service running was not simple. Disturbances encountered by Piry included Japan's annexation of Manchuria, an essential mail route to Europe; the plague of 1909–1910 which quarantined this same province; and the Chinese revolution of 1911. He did not anticipate the changes, and the fall of the empire took him by surprise. Like Hart before him, however, he was an authentic senior civil servant and managed to adjust his Service to circumstances. In November 1911, he was instructing his commissioner in Changsha (Hunan) to

> *Go on as you have on the footing of neutrality [. . .] the essential point is to work and maintain communications for the benefit of the public–and all parties irrespective of political colour* (Piry to Arlington, 9 November 1911, Letterbooks).[7]

During those years, the Pirys lived in Beijing. Isolation was a thing of the past since trains linked the capital with the port of Tianjin where all the comfortable amenities of Western life were available. Household orders to France became limited and irregular. Piry's letterbooks for the period deal with family matters, non-official Postal Service correspondence (official letters were treated by his secretaries), and, overwhelmingly, with photography.

THE PHOTOGRAPHS OF THE YUANMINGYUAN

Piry made twelve photographs of the European Palaces in 1876 and in 1911–13; they include the only color photographs of the site known for the period studied here. (To this may possibly be added the six Uslar-Durham prints seen above.) Because of their focus on a single subject, they reveal much about Piry's photographic development.

Figure 50. Picnic at the European Palaces: the Pirys and their friends by A.T. Piry. From a silver gelatin stereoscopic glass plate negative. Mrs. Piry stands at the rear right; her daughter Nalka turns her face to the camera on the foreground with Russian ambassador Korostovetz on her right.

The Nineteenth Century

The key photograph for the nineteenth century is a beautifully balanced view of the south facade of the palace (Fig. 16.) Six copies were traced,[8] but none is credited to Piry, and two are related to Ohlmer.

However, as discussed above, the Ohlmer lead is not conclusive. Much more serious is the Morse connection,[9] although it also is tortuous. In *The International Relations of the Chinese Empire* (1910), the former Customs Commissioner published two views of the European Palaces. The table states, "These two photographs taken about 1875, the first by Mr. Thomas Child, the second by M. A. Théophile Piry." This is erroneous; the second one is unmistakably Child's No. 204, the superb gate of the Aviary (Fig. 21.) And the "first" cannot be his: by 1876, Child was signing his plates, which is not the case here, and the style is too different from his usual work. On the opposite side, not only was Piry in Beijing when the image was created, but all the men involved, Morse, Piry, Ohlmer and Child, knew each other well. Friends exchange their work. A typographical error between "the first" and "the second" is thus the most reasonable explanation.

As a series of clues on which to base the attribution of Piry's preeminent photograph, this leaves something to be desired as crediting by default cannot be satisfactory. It is encouraging that several years of research later, nothing has appeared to invalidate this tentative conclusion. However, is there any evidence to prove that the Frenchman was a photographer by 1876?

The first formal indication is dated 28 January 1880 in Pakhoi when Piry mentioned receiving photographic material. The second is more precise still: an 1881 photograph shows a group of Inspectorate General men in Beijing. All are identified; looking tense, Piry sits on the far left. He holds in his hand a white air bulb attached to a tubing, the shutter pneumatic release. Undoubtedly, he is the photographer (Fig. 42.)

An earlier clue is even more dramatic. On the Chinese holiday of the fifth day of the fifth month (24 June 1879), Piry sailed from Pakhoi to Lianzhou (Hepu), where he set his camera and laboratory on the city walls. Possibly because his sympathy for the Christian missionaries was known, this innocent expedition "was construed as a preparation for choosing a site for a church, placards were issued, and a persecution began against the Chow (Zhou) family" (a Christian family with whom Piry and local missionaries used to stay when visiting). The unrest grew to such extent that the British consul in Pakhoi sent urgent messages to Beijing and in August summoned a cannonboat to protect foreign lives. The trouble faded at last, but the Chows lost all their property and were banished. Piry had attempted to discreetly intervene, but as a Chinese civil servant he could not take any direct action.[10]

While the riot the Frenchman unwittingly brought about is a striking illustration of the hazards of outdoor photography in China, it is also ample proof that he was an amateur photographer as early as 1879.

The Twentieth Century

The last ten photographs of the European Palaces are definitely Piry's, as they came directly from his daughter Jeanne to Charles Blackburn, his grandson.

They include three almost identical stereoscopic glass plates of a picnic along the north side of the reservoir of the Haiyantang. It is the only Western "everyday life" scene at the Yuanmingyuan, and a charming memento of leisure in Beijing at the end of the dynasty (Fig. 50.) The Pirys (minus the two boys at school in France) are seated with a group of companions. The Russian ambassador, Korostovetz, is on the right. This outing must have taken place during the autumn of 1911, just before Nalka, the youngest Piry daughter, eloped to Russia with the ambassador (G.E. Morrison:1 1976, 710–11). She sits in the forefront, turning her head back to look at the camera. Since the couple never returned to Beijing, the photograph cannot date after 1911.

The seven autochromes are very different. They are the only early color photographs of the site. Piry had immediately become enthusiastic for the Lumière brothers' invention. Sadly, the advent of color photography came too late for the European Palaces. The blues, purples, greens, whites and yellows of the glazed tiles described by the first visitors had long disappeared, torn off the walls and roofs by brick scavengers. Two panoramas show the staggering damage suffered by the garden since Ohlmer's photographs of 1873.

On another image, the Haiyantang serves as backdrop for the threshing of corn by a farmer and his water buffalo (Fig. 51.) The scene is autumnal, like the other Yuanmingyuan autochromes. A couple of Westerners standing on the stairs in the background provide a time frame. They were probably Isabelle Piry and the tall British diplomat she married in 1913, Arthur Blackburn. The scene should date between 1912, when Isabelle came back from Europe, and 1913; her parents were on their way to Paris before the summer of 1914. (They were back in Beijing for a few months in 1915–16, but with the war raging in Europe it is doubtful that Piry could then procure autochrome plates. The archives for the Lumière company are lost, so there is no forthcoming answer from that end either.)

THÉOPHILE PIRY, PHOTOGRAPHER

While few specimens of Piry's work before the 1900 fire of the Customs have survived, an impressive quantity of negatives and a few prints are known for the following years. Between the photographic documents and the letters, the family archives offer a detailed image of the photographer and his later work.

What stands out in the collection is the family group, and it is clear that frequent portrait sittings were an unescapable feature of life at the Pirys'. They fulfilled the two passions of the head of the household at the same time: his family and photography.

Piry bought good equipment and regularly tested new techniques, experimenting only for lack of ready-made solutions. Despite his optic and chemistry practical knowledge, he was not a scientist, but certainly a demanding and at times inventive craftsman for whom photography was a privileged means of expression.

Figure 51. Threshing corn near the Haiyantang, c. 1913. Stereoscopic autochrome by A.T. Piry.

Piry does not seem to have been a member of any photographic society. He did not exhibit his work or try to broadcast it. If a few rare samples were nevertheless published, this was due to circumstances, when his friends Morse and Ohlmer used a print he had given them or because his shots of the Siege of the Legations had such historical value it became a duty to use them (Laur 1904). (Many of his views of the Siege were indeed published uncredited through the years.)

The private character of Piry's photographs is confirmed by the overwhelming dominance in the collection of stereoscopic views. In fact, while the positive glass slides he made from his negatives, or the autochromes, were very effective through a stereoscope, they were small (4 x 4.4 or 4.1 per image) and their very principle was not suited to album collecting. Unfortunately for Post and Customs historians, Piry's professional life had no place in his photography. The few images taken of the Customs personnel (Beijing in 1881, Hart's garden-parties) were mere extensions of his private life.

With his marriage, Piry's favorite subjects had become his wife and children, his pride and universe. Friends came next, and strangers not at all. The absence of significant Chinese figures is especially striking. The picnic scene at the Yuanmingyuan is characteristic of a certain contemporary mode of life overseas, the only visible Chinese being the servants in the background. A high Chinese civil servant, fluent in the language, having lived in China much longer than in France,

Piry could have used as models his servants, his subalterns or his Chinese colleagues. He seems in fact to have done so in the early years, and also for a short while in 1901 in Beijing, where he photographed Chinese daily life. The oldest album preserved (1886–88), from Korea, shows his neighbors and Japanese servants or a few Korean officials in his home. But the scenery is limited to his garden, literally. Piry's photographic work can be summarized in two subjects which were closely related: his family, and its extension *Le Rodoir*, the estate in Britanny he purchased in 1903 and which he photographed, quite literally, tree by tree. Unique among the photographers studied, this limitation, or obsession, is an unlikely context for images of the European Palaces.

Still, depending on the period considered (nineteenth or twentieth century), there are two possible justifications for Piry's views of the European Palaces. As a single man in Beijing in 1877, he was taking part in all activities providing relief from the monotony of daily life, among which country outings and picnics were an important part. It was also natural for a novice photographer to try his technique on monuments of unquestionable historical importance. Likewise, it was his later passion for color photography which generated his 1913 autochromes of the European Palaces: although he tried various solutions to reduce the autochrome's long exposure time, he reluctantly had to revert to the still life compositions of his early years when using color plates. Thirty years after Child, he went to the same places, partly for the same reason: monuments do not move and can therefore be exposed with a slow emulsion.

Color photography was the object of most of Piry's photographic correspondence during his last years in Beijing. His creative attempts to procure autochrome plates would have wide-ranging repercussions.

Unprocessed autochromes had only a short life, and even worse, they fared poorly in humid heat. The normal route for parcels from France through the Suez canal took several weeks in tropical areas, and Piry found it inadequate for his purposes. As the newly opened Trans-Siberian railway carried only letters between France and China, for a time the Frenchman had Lumière mail a few plates at a time in an envelope. Then, in February 1910, he started a new system through the German postal service whereby Lumière shipped to an address in Germany a five-kilo parcel post already wrapped and addressed to Piry in Beijing. The transaction was repeated a number of times. Soon, all the plates and photographic equipment went the same route.[11]

On 25 September 1911, Piry wrote to Lumière:

> *I am sending you a special note on the way to ship [parcel post] through the "Berliner Speditur Verein, in Berlin" [. . .] In my quality as postmaster general, I personally made all arrangements with this agency, & this shipping route is open to all your clients in China.*

This is how the Postmaster General's passion for color photography generated a new international postal service between France and China.

FROM THE BOXER REBELLION TO THE WARLORDS

11. ALFONS FREIHERR MUMM VON SCHWARZENSTEIN A German Envoy in 1901 China

In 1902, there was published in Berlin an oblong photographic album bound in leather and cloth, with the single title, *Ein Tagebuch in Bildern* ("A Diary in Pictures") in the center, and a bright coat-of-arms on the top left corner. The title page was a dedication in flowery gothic print:

> *To my collaborators in Peking (Beijing), in friendly recollection from your chief Alfons von Mumm, Imperial Envoy Extraordinary and Minister Plenipotentiary.*

A four-clawed Chinese dragon and the number in the limited edition completed the page. The author was an amateur photographer, the German Minister in Beijing.[1]

ALFONS FREIHERR MUMM VON SCHWARZENSTEIN (1859–1924)

Alfons von Mumm, or, to give him his full name and title, Alfons Freiherr Mumm von Schwarzenstein, was German Minister in two major East Asia countries, China (1900–1906) and Japan (1906–1911).[2] He was brought to China by the 1900 Boxer Rebellion, appointed to replace Baron von Ketteler who had been murdered by the Boxers.

While in office, he saw the end of the Boxer Rebellion, the emergence of Japan as a world power and Japan's incredible (for Westerners) crushing military victory over Russia. He left East Asia only a few months before the Revolution which was to bring down the last Chinese dynasty.

Mumm was forty-one years old when he arrived from Germany with the relief forces. A law doctor, he had entered the diplomatic service in 1885 and had never been in East Asia before. He travelled to China with the German relief forces, arriving in Shanghai shortly after the Beijing Legations had been relieved in August 1900. He retired from his position as Minister in Tokyo in 1911, married a Scottish lady and lived in Italy until his death in 1924. His personality remains obscure, as does his photographic experience before 1900.

The envoy's portraits show an amiable and unpretentious man. He was indeed to be remembered in Beijing as a genial host keeping the best table in the capital. Although younger than most of his colleagues, he proved very successful in these complicated times. Mumm served his country well, the intransigence of his position being noted on several occasions, and Germany's influence in that part of the world was strengthened by the new treaties.

EIN TAGEBUCH IN BILDERN

Ein Tagebuch in Bildern accompanied Mumm between July 1900 and 1902, from Genoa in Italy to Shanghai, Tianjin, and Beijing where he first arrived on 21 October 1900. Following his exploration of the city and its surrounding attractions, more distant excursions were made north to the Great Wall or Jehol (now Chengde). Then the Minister went on tour of inspection of the German consulates on the Chinese coast in 1901, before returning to Beijing. The layout of the album is informal: the images vary in size, some are straight, some slanted; many are captioned but some not; they are arranged by topic. There are two hundred sixty-seven plates, over five hundred pictures, sometimes touched up for better contrast.

What Mumm saw were the common people met in roadside inns, the blood princes, the conquerors' parades in the Forbidden City. It was also the image of a civilization he honored through multiple views of temples and palaces. If the diplomat acknowledged in his foreword that his official position allowed him access to previously inaccessible sites or to Western and Chinese officials, his function was not otherwise significant. In addition, he observed without attempting analysis. Leaving behind the demonstrative and didactic nineteenth century, he took his place in the twentieth century, more neutral and respectful of differences. However, Mumm, the photographer, was still a nineteenth century man inasmuch as he did not try for the framing or light effects which would soon become commonplace even for amateur photographers.

Mumm used a portable camera, presumably with glass plates.[3] In the quarter of a century between Child and Mumm, a revolution of photography had taken place at the technical level, and would soon occur culturally as well. Freed from technical constraints, the "amateur" would, from then on, produce work different from the professional's. The spontaneousness afforded by the new camera is very clear in the fourth chapter, "My travels in the country."

The diplomat did the usual outings north toward and beyond the Great Wall, a vacation. As for south China, he went there on an official tour of inspection of the German consulates along the coast. This was both a state and an unpretentious affair, travelling on a German warship with the head of the German fleet, yet being entertained by amateur theatricals . . .[4]

When did the Minister find the time to shoot all these photographs? The diplomatic agenda was busy in post-Boxer Rebellion Beijing. His two-page foreword tells us this and more. In a tiny spidery gothic handwriting, Mumm explained that "the greater part [of the photographs] were taken by myself, a smaller number on my orders by my valet Anton Goebel," since he himself had "little leisure" to indulge in his "old hobby of photography." Mumm was barely fifteen months in Beijing before the manuscript was sent to Berlin. So either Goebel was more active a partner than is acknowledged, or His Excellency must have had some leisure despite the demanding diplomatic activity he complained about.

As a matter of fact, there is more to it; some (uncredited) photographs in the book were made long before either man arrived in China.[5] Nevertheless, they are not misplaced amongst the later work. In 1901, old China was still everywhere to be seen, side by side with the ruins left by the Beijing or Tianjin Sieges, or even in the Forbidden City while it was being used for the review of foreign troops. In fact, whoever made the photographs is somewhat unimportant: Mumm chose to publish them with his own—or Goebel's—work, and made the book a whole.

Figure 52. Feldmarschal Graf Waldersee in Beijing, c. 1900, by A. Mumm von Schwarzenstein. *Ein Tagebuch in Bildern*, 134.

This bizarre creative association, between a turn-of-the-century servant and a German aristocrat belonging to a corps whose conservatism and class consciousness are still bywords today, reminds us of the French millionaire Albert Kahn who in 1908 sent his chauffeur for a crash course in photography before taking him on a trip round the world.[6] Passion for a common subject has always erased some barriers, at least in private. What is more noteworthy is the public recognition of such a relationship.

The resulting book is a fascinating document on a world and a man both long since gone. The world is there for everyone to see, in the palaces and street scenes, the military parades and the landscapes; here is eternal China apparently inured to the passing of time in its streets and courtyards, wounded China of 1901 subjected to Foreign will . . . The man is more elusive. An educated German, he was sensitive to the poetry of old stones and buildings and also appreciative—with "suitable" condescension—of the exoticism of the Chinese way of life. He was nationalist, quite superior, and certainly interested in symbols (so many occasions for parades in the Forbidden City, the ultimate humiliation!) In fact, we find a man very much of his time.

Mumm is present on every page. He travelled towards a country in turmoil where he would have huge responsibilities, still recording his trip as any worry-free traveller would have done. He settled into everyday life as he framed his subjects in the streets and courtyards. For all his Western prejudices against China—and these were particularly strong in the world at large in the aftermath of the Boxer Rebellion, Mumm did not show the Chinese at a disadvantage. A singularity of the book is the absence of any stereotype. He captured a country wounded by war, but omitted the massacres which were for many contemporary photographers the occasion to underline Chinese "barbarity." He did not try to make a point, but described what he liked. The brutal vision of China commonly spread about was very different, centered on blood and destruction.[7]

Facets of Mumm's personality are revealed here and there in the album. He was a true diplomat. In the Forbidden City, the British are courteously presented before the Germans, as they had been in Beijing longer. French troops show off the old Cathedral built by their missionaries. Certainly, there are more photographs of Germans than of other nationals, but Field Marshall Count Waldersee, the Commander-in-Chief of the allied troops, obviously deserved a full page (Fig. 52). Mumm was also thorough and systematic (no major site in or around Peking was ignored), and sometimes romantic (his German mind was drawn to the special atmosphere of the ruined European Palaces (182–85), ignored by most photographers.) There is a definite sense of majesty in the book's many architectural views, yet the same impressive quality can be found in the few formal portraits.

The Minister's album is not everyone's. Few books actually offer so much diversity. The splendidly framed temples at Jehol (Chengde) delight the eye, while the incongruity of the high born Imperial prince, keeper of the Xiling (Western) Imperial tombs, posing arm-in-arm with two Westerners (206, top left), is fully appreciated. The photographs are meant to speak for themselves, to be striking, and they are.

12. FROM THE 1911 REVOLUTION TO THE WARLORDS

The second important group of photographers of the European Palaces was active during the years 1911–1925.[1] Throughout this deeply troubled period which started with the fall of the Empire and the emergence of the Republic, continued with the confiscation of the latter by Warlords and concluded with the 1925 death of Sun Wen (Sun Yat-sen), numbers of foreigners were attracted to Beijing. Besides an active intellectual and cosmopolitan life, the capital now boasted photographic shops and studios; for visitors and Chinese alike, the practice and collection of photography had become a fact of life.

With the abdication of the last Qing emperor in 1912, the European Palaces had at last become fully accessible. In the following years, five series of significant photographs of the site were gathered by new Western visitors. These included Conrad Anner, Carl Whiting Bishop, Sophus Black, Osvald Sirén, and a Mr. Alimoff whose first name was never recorded; together, they produced a total of ninety-five images.

They were men who would distinguish themselves in fields all related to China, but far removed from photography and the European Palaces. This research identified them between 1987 and 1990 as photographers of the Yuanmingyuan. Because the subject was circumscribed to only a few buildings over fourteen years, cross-referencing the collections reached a level rarely possible in studies of early twentieth century photography in China. While providing answers, this also highlighted the problems attached to a joint representation of this, or any, architectural group. In addition, as the more problematic series were the last to be found, each successive conclusion contradicted the previous ones. The final name, Anner's, was in fact the determining factor in the final balance of the entire group; it also comes early in the alphabetical order.

THE INDIVIDUALS

Alimoff, the Unknown

In 1946, the Musée Guimet in Paris received from a Mr. Alimoff a set of eight photographs of the European Palaces. The prints bear on the back a short manuscript description and a number. One also states, "printed in 1922." Nothing further is known of this series or its author. The condition of the site tallies with the date given.

Conrad W. Anner (1889–1960), Architect: Collector or Photographer?

The Conrad W. Anner papers in the Rockefeller Archive Center in North Tarrytown, New York state, include twenty-nine photographs of the European Palaces. This is the largest collection dated before 1925, as well as a crucial reference for all the images of the period. They were found listed by Archie Crouch, *et al.* (1989) as photographs of the "Old Summer Palace." The three weeks following this discovery in December 1990 saw an intensive exchange of letters and photocopies with the Center's archivist and the application for a research grant followed, eight months later, by a two-week visit. At that time, the four other series for the period were known; it immediately became clear that Anner's collection was going to totally upset the previous painstaking conclusions.

Conrad Anner was born in 1889 to Swiss parents in Berlin where his father was a pastor.[2] He emigrated to the United States in 1909 with a degree in architecture.

Figure 53. Imperial officials in the Forbidden City after 1911, Anner Collection. Also published by Enders (187).

In 1919, he was sent to Beijing by the Rockefeller Foundation, to work on the construction of the Peking Union Medical College.[3] He became architect-in-charge of the project in 1923. He also assisted in other projects sponsored by the Foundation, such as the building of the National Library of Beijing and the restoration of the Palace Museum. This is how he received a key and free access to the Forbidden City.[4]

Anner returned to the United States in 1931 after the Medical College's completion. He was involved in the restoration of the colonial town of Williamsburg, Virginia, and then worked for the U.S. government. This is the reason why he went back to Beijing after the Second World War to restore the buildings of the U.S. embassy. As the city was overrun by the Communists in 1949, he was evacuated along with the diplomatic personnel; the plane landed in a street cleared of its trees.[5] After this, Anner continued to work in Asia for several years. He died in 1960, and the Rockefeller Archive Center acquired from Mrs. Anner part of his personal archives, including photographs of China and Thailand.

The European Palaces series belongs to a collection of over one thousand photographic prints and three hundred fifty glass slides gathered in China before 1930 by Anner. There are numerous images of construction in progress at the Medical College, as well as various architectural views and street scenes. Most prints are anonymous, vary in size and shape, and are mounted on loose grey cardboard sheets.

The Anner series on the European Palaces stands out both for sheer quantity and for its emphasis on architectural technique. It includes photographs of the site as well as of the twenty 1783 engravings of the European Palaces.[6] Overall, in importance as a subject, the Yuanmingyuan comes immediately after the Medical College. There are four tinted glass slides (two of which exist also in print form), and twenty-seven prints of the palaces, of a format different from all other Anner prints (see pp. 139–142.)

Inconsistencies abound. The haphazard grouping of the photographs, which does not respect either the layout or even the unity of a particular building, is disturbing. While Anner was certainly a photographer (his wife has slides of Thailand taken by him in the 1950s), his authorship of at least the greater portion of the Yuanmingyuan photographs is questionable. It now appears that they were made before his arrival in 1919.

There are two formats of prints. One, small and squarish, includes eight examples for which no information could be found. But the other twenty, larger and wider, lead to very interesting developments.

Three of them were used in 1966 in a German doctoral thesis on the European Palaces by Alexander Schulz; the source was the manuscript thesis presented in 1915 in Beijing by one Tsao Muh Tuh [sic].[7] Another view was published by Friedrich Perzynski in 1920, still too early for Anner to have provided it[8].

Ten Anner prints are numbered in the lower right corner with three digits handwritten on the negative. Such a serial number is found on images of the European Palaces outside the Anner collection; all numbers stand between 536 and 559.[9] As, in addition, there are no other numbered photographs in the Anner collection, it is unlikely that the numbers refer to the collection. Is this a much larger suite of photographs (at least 559 numbers) for which the author, nature and size are still to be determined?[10]

The numbered views of the Yuanmingyuan cannot be later than 1915, the year Tsao defended his thesis, and they could be older still. Perzynski went to China in 1912–1913, when he probably collected his prints.[11]

In addition, seven of the non-Yuanmingyuan Anner photographs are found credited to one William Allen Dunn (Enders 1923).[12] Hence the conclusion that, if this Yuanmingyuan photographer—or photographers—was apparently not Anner himself, he could have been Dunn, or just as easily a Chinese, possibly Tsao Muh Tuh or a professional. This would open the new perspective of the images of the European Palaces made by Chinese photographers.

As to Anner's interest in the European Palaces, it is less mysterious. Just like the Jesuits' earlier creations, the Peking Union Medical College was a group of buildings combining architectural styles. The structure and walls were Western, but the galleries and roofs were Chinese, while the auditorium was given the appearance of a Confucian temple. The similitude cannot have escaped the architect's attention.

There could be more to it, however. Anner himself admitted to being more interested in the mechanics of things than in their aesthetics (*Curriculum Vitae* 1931). He had designed the technical aspects of the College: generator, heating system and laboratories. Was the famous hydraulic system created by Father Benoist for the European Palaces an added attraction? On this, the selection of views does not permit a definitive answer.

Carl Whiting Bishop (1881–1942), Archeologist

Carl W. Bishop, born and raised in Tokyo in a Protestant missionary family, studied anthropology in the United States. In 1915, while an assistant curator in the new Department of Far Eastern Art in the University Museum, University of Pennsylvania in Philadelphia, he was sent on an archeological mission to North China (1915–1917) (*Museum Journal* March 1915, 83). From 1918 to 1920, he was with the United States Navy as an assistant naval attaché in China. Then in 1923–27, he led there another archeological mission sponsored by the Freer Gallery in Washington and the Boston Museum of Fine Arts. His last mission in China took place in 1929–1934, under the auspices of the Freer Gallery, when he took part in important archeological excavations at the Neolithic period site of Wanquanxian (Shanxi) and at the Shang Dynasty site of Anyang (Henan) (Goodrich "Carl Whiting Bishop," Carl W. Bishop papers, FGA).

Bishop made extensive use of photography for his records. Four thousand negatives he made in China are in the archives of the Freer Gallery. They include twenty-three views of the European Palaces; several are rare and valuable panoramas of the site.

At the time of Bishop's first visit in 1915, the large North American museums were mounting their own field expeditions to develop their collections.[13] The archeologist's assignment was to conduct excavations in order to provide the University Museum with archeological objects.[14] He was also instructed to procure ethnographical objects and books for the library.

However, although spending almost three years in East Asia, Bishop never managed to do any archaeological field work. In 1917 alone, floods cut all access routes between Beijing and the provinces, after troubles so serious that the capital was the object of direct confrontations between warlords. This is how Bishop's diary entry for 1 July 1917 read:

> *Took a ride in a.m. Surprised to see all the streets and shop fronts displaying the old dragon flag; found out that Chang Hsün [Zhang Xun] had restored the Manchu dynasty early this morning.*

The restoration lasted only a few days, but there was fighting at the Temple of Heaven. Setting up expeditions in such a context was naturally unthinkable.

The American spent his enforced sojourns in the capital learning Chinese, making useful contacts, and carrying his camera everywhere. On 28 August 1915, he wrote to George B. Gordon, the University Museum director,

> *In the interval of my calling upon people here I have found time to visit and photograph most of the points of interest in Peking and its immediate vicinity. Among the points I have visited are [. . .] the old and new Summer Palaces . . .*

He added,

> *I had also planned a few short trips [to the Great wall, etc.], but unfortunately the rainy season is just now at its height, and camping trips are out of the question.*

The letter further indicated that Bishop was using the darkroom of the friend who housed him and helped him print the quantity of photographs taken since his arrival in China. His diary tells of daily visits to the photographic shops of Hartung's and Camera Craft's, and of the work they did for him.

His expense account, very detailed, offers two possible dates for the trip to the Yuanmingyuan. He wrote on 18 August, "$1,20, Rikis [rickshaws] to Temple of

Figure 54. Eastward view toward the Yuanyingguan from the Haiyantang, c. 1915, by C.W. Bishop. From silver gelatin celluloid rollfilm.

Heaven, etc.," and on 22 August "$1,00, Rikis about suburbs." The second outing was probably when he recorded the European Palaces. This was Bishop's only documented visit to the site, although he returned a few years later.

Why would photographs taken during a mission financed by the University of Pennsylvania be found in a national museum in Washington? We can hazard a guess based on the sequence of events. Bishop, sent to China with a research program at least broadly defined, had accomplished only a small part of it after two and a half years. While he had actually purchased books for the library and a number of Chinese and Japanese objects which are now in the University Museum,[15] he had also spent most of his time in Beijing and had never done any of the excavating his employers considered the primary purpose of his mission. Upon receiving the detailed accounts of his activities, the Board of Directors may have felt that Bishop had priorities different from their own. He was indeed insisting on his progress in Chinese and on his photographic work.[16] Repeated statements on the impossibility of starting to excavate for lack of a competent Chinese assistant (in 1915), then because of the cycle of political unrest and natural disasters, seem to have exhausted the Board's patience. The Bishop Papers include a letter from a "specialist" stating that winter, being a dry season in north China, was the best time to conduct archeological field work. Considering the very harsh weather Bishop was experiencing first-hand, his position could only be the opposite.

Recalled to Philadelphia, he left China in early January 1918. His draft by the U.S. Navy concluded a divorce that was certainly stormy. The Museum entered at that time in its collection items "found in Mr. Bishop's office," a formula suggesting he could not even recover his personal belongings.[17] While the Museum archives contain a few photographs taken by the Bishop mission, the archeologist left to the Freer Gallery the negatives he had described in his diaries and letters as well as their careful indexing. (Incidentally, his dealings with the Freer were also difficult, and his first mission to China (1923–1927) under this new patronage was barely more successful than the previous one on a purely archeological level. However, it was under the Freer's name that Bishop finally undertook important excavations, wrote most of his work, and gained an international reputation.[18])

Nothing among Bishop's notes or publications gives the slightest indication of a personal interest in the European Palaces.

Sophus Black (1882–1960), Telegraph Manager

Born in 1882 in Marstal, Denmark, Sophus Black was given a double entry in the *Dansk Biografisk Leksikon* (Bind 1979, 210), as manager of telegraphs and art collector. During his twenty-nine years in China (1902–1931) with the Great Northern Telegraph Company, a Danish company, he acquired a deserved reputation as a Chinese art collector.

He arrived in 1907 in Beijing where in 1915 he married Minna Dich, a goldsmith. The couple lived in a Chinese house, having, as was then deeply frowned upon, "gone native" by adopting a Chinese way of life. Black knew the language, and acquired from the capital's antique dealers an important collection of religious paint-

Figure 55. Yuanyingguan, east, central niche, c. 1915, by S. Black.

ings, mostly Buddhist. He had close ties with the National Museum of Denmark in Copenhagen, which eventually received or acquired his collection.

Black's twenty photographs of the European Palaces in the Department of Ethnology of the National Museum are his only photographs in the collections, and are not documented (Hornby 1986 and personal communications). They could have been a complement to his set of 1783 engravings of the palaces now also in the Museum. Were the photographs a comparison between the former state of the garden and the distressing reality? Whatever the case, they certainly testify to a personal interest in the European Palaces.

Osvald Sirén (1879–1966), Art Historian

Black's fellow Scandinavian, Osvald Sirén, is without doubt the photographer of the European Palaces best known among sinologists. He studied them in two different works, *Palaces of Peking* and *Gardens of China*, publishing nine images in all. The Östasiatiska Museet in Stockholm, Sweden, has eight more views in the Sirén archives (see pp. 158–9).

Sirén was born in 1879 in Helsinki, Finland, and became the first professor of the history of fine arts at Stockholm University.[19] A noted authority on Italian painting, his interest turned to Far Eastern art in 1916–17 when he lectured at both Yale and Harvard Universities in the United States. Later, he travelled extensively in China and Japan for study and collection. From 1928 to 1945, Sirén was Keeper of pictures and sculptures at the National Museum in Stockholm, for which he built up a collection of Chinese paintings and sculptures. He visited notable Oriental art collections the world over and widely published the results of his studies. He produced several major works on the history of Chinese art, Chinese sculpture and Chinese painting, as well as a staggering number of articles in several languages; the publications listed on the occasion of his eightieth birthday ran to four hundred sixty-five references. Upon his death, he left his art library and over 10,000 photographs to the University of Helsinki, where he had studied and taught. The photographs and related archives, now in the Östasiatiska Museet in Stockholm, have not yet been published.[20]

Sirén's study of the European Palaces was not done in any depth, nor was it very positive. He stated in *Gardens of China*,

> *The task of the Jesuit artist was [. . .] to create as rich and pompous a picture of foreign architecture as possible.*

He went on:

> *As these rather curious, not to say hybrid, establishments are of no particular interest for our special study [on Chinese gardens], only enough examples will be presented to give an idea of the style of the buildings* (Sirén 1949, 127).

Sirén seems to have included the subject only as a part of the whole Summer Palace. Still, his point that "there was no question of any deliberate adaptation of the buildings to the milieu" (1949, 128) highlights the essential difference between the Chinese and the Western areas of the Yuanmingyuan.

Sirén used photography extensively and well, and in a modern way which saw the image as a reference as well as a research aid. There is some indication of his method of operation in his 1924 article "A Chinese Emperor Plays Photographic Assistant" describing a shooting session inside the Forbidden City in 1922 with the young ex-emperor Xuantong (Puyi) in attendance.

THE GROUP OF PHOTOGRAPHS

The study of these ninety-five late photographs of the European Palaces was eventful, at times presenting all the hazards of the erection and preservation of a house of cards. It happens that the five series discussed above include all but a handful of the images traced for the period. Month after month, each new find was integrated into the collection and the whole constantly reassessed in light of the new information. Datings were attempted, both relative (between prints), and absolute (inside the time frame that kept being redefined). By the end of 1990, the chronology thus established put Black, Sirén, Bishop and Alimoff in that order, and between c. 1919 and c. 1922.

As could be expected when dealing with such elusive and incomplete material, there were discrepancies. However, the whole was workable and provided the possibility of a decent amalgamation of the information. In addition, repeats of views between series were more common than for the 1870s—although not quite enough, as it finally turned out.

There were unexpected pitfalls, as some crucial information proved erroneous. Precise inquiries finally revealed that the date "1915" attached to Black was nothing more than the half-way mark of his stay in China. Worse, Bishop had been in Beijing in 1915 (Goodrich "Carl Whiting Bishop," Carl W. Bishop papers, FGA), eight years earlier than previously assumed. (This last find upset the whole chronology of the four series then available.) The only stable date was Alimoff; this could hardly be considered positive, as nothing more ever came to light about him or his photographs.

The real turning point was the discovery of Anner's collection in December 1990. The new pictures highlighted discrepancies in the chronology of the sixty-six views to that date. Documenting the period, and not merely the Yuanmingyuan, became imperative. A trip to Philadelphia yielded essential details from Bishop's papers, while views from the Anner series were found outside the Rockefeller Archives. Suddenly, everything seemed to fall into place. (Surprisingly, and, one could almost say, revoltingly, the c. 1915 date for the Sophus Black set found itself confirmed.) The final conclusions seem to stand on sound foundations. The researcher's experience suggests, however, that adjustments will take place if, and when, additional documents come to light.

*
* *

As a whole or isolated, the five sets for the period 1911–1925 are in every respect different from the nineteenth century production. First, they are more numerous, with a total of ninety-five views against forty-three. Second, they show the garden in a much more dilapidated condition. Finally, the images alone do not provide a chronology; in contrast, the large clear views of the Xieqiqu from the previous century had left no room for doubt despite their spanning a mere five years.

Sadly, the quality is also generally inferior. This is a consequence of photographic progress; anyone could now make photographs, whether talented or not. In these series, some framing is erratic and images are out of focus. The size of the prints is also less than one-fifth that of Ohlmer's. Even enlarged, they cannot compete for clarity of detail. On the other hand, the photographs were made from closer up or from places previously unreachable—indeed, an outstanding view was shot from the top of a high wall of the Xieqiqu, clearly outlining the pavement and the polylobed basin (Fig. 56.)

In addition, the very subject matter of the photographs changed. The post-1911 period saw a shift from monument to detail, a clear reflection of the ongoing decay. In 1901 still, Mumm had stood at a distance; post-1925 photographers would single out details because no worthwhile structures remained intact.

A period of relative calm between two great waves of destruction, the years 1911–1924 were kind to the ruins of the European Palaces. Because of this, views taken over a decade by different people are surprisingly similar. Indeed, establishing a chronology relying only on the six comparable images of the Aviary Gate proved impossible: what little facings and decorative elements remained by 1911 (Anner) were still there in 1922 (Sirén), and any changes in the brick core were so slight that nothing significantly distinguishes these views.

Less damaged structures were more reliable and the coating on the surface was a good clue. Valueless to scavengers, it remained when facings had been ripped

Figure 56. South of Xieqiqu from top c. 1911. Anner Collection.

off. Graffiti were also taken into account, although they were less reliable as most were painted and paint washes off. They are Chinese characters (anti-Western slogans) or numbers.[21]

Just as the Xieqiqu had been the best instrument of comparison forty years earlier, the Yuanyingguan now became the basic reference. With the removal of the outside wall, the palace was accessible on its four sides. In fact, two distant views of it ultimately proved that Bishop had made two distinct series several years apart, which contradicted his own archive inventory dating all the photographs of the palaces to 1915.

Based on all data available, the final conclusion is that the 1911–1925 views were made in the following order: Anner, c. 1911–2; Bishop ("wide"), 1915; Black, c. 1915–1918; Alimoff, 1922; Sirén, 1922; and Bishop ("square"), c. 1923–1925. In the end, biographical data had failed to properly document these five photographers' individual activities in Beijing, but in-depth study of the images they had created of a single place had provided the answers.

*

* *

For reasons peculiar to the history of China, the Alimoff, Anner, Bishop, Black and Sirén photographs were the last coherent images of a vanishing architecture. It is probably human nature that things appear precious only when there is no longer any hope of saving them. The years that followed the fall of the Qing empire saw an increasing awareness of the historical and artistic value of the European Palaces. This was too little, and too late, to influence their fate.

CONCLUSION

THE PHOTOGRAPHERS OF THE EUROPEAN PALACES, GROUP OR INDIVIDUALS?

It cannot be denied that, as a source, the photographs of the European Palaces should be studied together. On the other hand, to claim that the photographers themselves form a cohesive group would be unrealistic.

In fact, any connections between them seem weak at best. It is clear that Child, Ohlmer and Piry were in close contact in Beijing for some time, but only the last two men kept in touch into the 1880s (Piry Letterbooks). Child, who went back home in 1879, met none of the later photographers. Piry photographed Mumm on the occasion of the signing of the 1901 treaties and they both moved in the same circles for five years. Ohlmer was then in Qingdao; a senior Customs officer and a German, he certainly had opportunities to meet both Piry and Mumm.

Among the twentieth century photographers, Black, a reputed art collector, lived longest in Beijing. One can assume that he met Anner, a long-time resident also attracted to China and its art. Sirén, another Scandinavian and an art scholar, is likely to have come in contact with him also. All this, however, is guesswork. While Bishop, a fellow American to Anner, was apparently in Beijing at the same time as Sirén, it is not established that the two men knew each other at the time their respective photographs were made.[1]

In fact, the only certain common ground between the members of the group is photography. With 1900 and the real opening of the city, specialized shops were established in Beijing. This is how, between 1933 and 1938, the German Hedda (Hammer) Morrison was in charge of the famous Hartung Photo Shop. However, chance and the then harrowing times mean that none of the photographers of the European Palaces was still in Beijing when she arrived. Ohlmer, Piry and Mumm were dead; Anner and Black had just returned home, following Perckhammer (see p. 151 n. 2). Hedda Morrison remained alone, with her friend, the writer/art historian George Kates, to enjoy the peculiar charm of the ruined palaces. When she photographed them, it was more to confirm their radical fall from grace than to transmit the image of a paradise, by then only a distant memory.

*

* *

Nevertheless, the photographers of the Yuanmingyuan between 1873 and 1925 had features in common.[2] Even considering the shortage of significant and/or comprehensive information, several trends are clear. First, the photographs were made by men, and young men in particular; this, however, only reflects the foreign population of China at the time, and is not significant. More interestingly, almost all of them were long-term residents; if they often visited the site early in their stay (Mumm in 1901, Bishop in 1915), they intended to remain for a number of years, and most learned the spoken language at least. In addition, four shared a German background and culture. Amateur photographers were also preeminent among them, which could confirm that the general lack of interest in the European Palaces prevented photographs of the site from being a worthwhile commercial investment. The existing views, therefore, were essentially personal records, with the consequence that they were never commonly available.[3]

Still, only eleven Western photographers of the European Palaces could be identified for the years 1860–1925. This is astonishingly little at a time when photography showed *ad nauseam* images of "exotic" countries, and Beijing at large was extensively covered by both amateur and professional practitioners. The problematic access to the garden, particularly before 1900, may have been a factor, but it is not sufficient as an explanation, as the relative shunning of the site went on well into the twentieth century when the gardens—or what was left of them—had become totally accessible to visitors.

Was the disinterest of Western photographers related to the dubious circumstances of the destruction of the Yuanmingyuan? For a long time, the British and French had the largest contingent of visitors to Beijing, yet only one of the photographers was French, and one British.

Most often, photography of ruins in China was limited to the aftermath of the destruction. The recurrent and well-known images of the burned shell of the Tianjin cathedral where nuns and converts were massacred in 1870, belong to a different type. They were used as testimony to the barbarity of Chinese mobs against innocent missionaries, a highly charged emotional and political theme. In fact, similar photographs of the devastation wrought by foreigners on the Yuanmingyuan during the same period would have meant attacking Europe's "barbarity," a difficult proposition for Westerners. As seen with Ohlmer's 1898 comments, there was on the opposite a marked tendency among those interested visitors toward emphasizing the construction, rather than the destruction, of the palaces. Although most authors continued to bemoan the Yuanmingyuan's destruction, many also believed it had been a political necessity, and few made an issue of it.

This is a complicated matter. For example, there is no doubt that the nearby garden of Wanshoushan (site of the new Summer Palace, the Yiheyuan), also damaged by fire in 1860, was often photographed by foreigners. There, however, some magnificent Chinese architecture had remained untouched, and photographers did not show the truly ruined areas. So, was it fine to photograph places torched by the Western armies in 1860, so long as the damage was not devastation? But in 1873 this could also be said of most of the European Palaces enclosure.

In fact, rejection of an architecture where no element was fully Chinese nor totally Western, was probably the most important factor. And the Bund at Shanghai, symbol of imperialistic superiority and a Western showpiece, was much more popular than the European Palaces, with their more ambiguous style and symbolic taint.

For the answering perspective, one should also wonder what it was that attracted those photographers who came. In particular, four Germans out of eleven photographers is a high percentage: here the peculiarly ornate style of the palaces appears to have played a crucial role. The predominant Baroque style belonged to a tradition long deprecated in most Western countries. But the Germanic countries continued to admire it long after it had gone out of fashion elsewhere. The extraordinary saga of the palaces was probably seen as an added attraction, as was the romantic ruined effect that so impressed Ohlmer.

THE CONTRIBUTION OF THE EUROPEAN PALACES PHOTOGRAPHERS TO THE KNOWLEDGE OF TRADITIONAL CHINA

Beyond their interest in the European Palaces, the photographers of the European Palaces also shared an unconventional vision of the country and its people. None of them produced those "exotic" photographs ubiquitously found in albums. The three "necessary" views of China collected in so many travel albums—bound feet, torture/execution and opium—were not for them. Child and Ohlmer recorded their surroundings, whether buildings or people; Piry was a family photographer, devoid of any clear opinion on China and the Chinese; the twentieth century started with Mumm, who showed refreshing restraint in applying to China the Western moral and social criteria of his time. Then, a shift towards acknowledging China as a valuable civilization soon became visible with Anner and Perckhammer, and even more so later with Morrison. Bishop and Sirén were still between two worlds, their photographs a kind of scientific note in image, in line with, if not in the spirit of, the nineteenth century.

The contribution of these men to the knowledge of China in their time goes far beyond photography. Nevertheless, Child is remembered for his important corpus of views of Beijing made between 1870 and 1889. Together with Ernst von Perckhammer (about 1915) and Hedda Morrison (in Beijing 1933–1946), he fixed for future generations the image of a disappearing mode of life and social order. After him, the new Summer Palace of Yiheyuan/Wanshoushan was rebuilt and enlarged by the Dowager Empress, sacked again in 1900 and again rebuilt. On the eve of the effective destruction of the China of old and of its spirit, Hedda Morrison captured the faces and sites of Beijing in images reflecting her deep knowledge and understanding of the people. A few years earlier, Perckhammer had highlighted the monuments and the people of Beijing as they appeared to a visiting photographic artist.

The work in China of Mumm von Schwarzenstein is twofold. His album belongs to the photographic history of the China that was, but he also significantly furthered the imperialistic interests of his country with the treaties which followed the Boxer Rebellion. As for Sirén, his contribution to the study of Chinese art and architecture is well known. Chinese studies were his life's work, and his publications on architecture, sculpture and painting are still current.

None of the other photographers of the Yuanmingyuan made a name in photography. Furthermore, in various ways, their professional obligations were aimed at forcing China into modern times. Still, they also contributed to Chinese studies. Ernst Ohlmer published several articles on the Qingdao Customs system as well as an early German-language catalog on ceramics. The porcelain collection he gave the Roemer-Pelizaeus Museum in Hildesheim remains important. Also a collector, Sophus Black was instrumental in developing the collections of Buddhist paintings in the National Museum of Copenhagen. Together with Sirén in Stockholm, these men provided an impetus that developed centers of expertise in Northern Europe. In the same way, Carl W. Bishop's work belongs to the history of Chinese archeology, while his collecting is the pride of several U.S. museums.

Théophile Piry is a unique case. Among his views of China, such as they were found, the Beijing autochromes are the important part, and more so maybe for history of photography than for history of China. Yet, his views of the 1900 Siege and of the streets of Beijing in 1901 should no more be discounted than his daily chronicle of Western family life in China. Nevertheless, his life achievement remains the development of the Chinese Postal Service, a project most certainly oriented towards the future.

That Conrad Anner contributed his important architectural work on the Peking Union Medical College to the advancement of medicine in China, must not hide his contribution to other projects. Bound to modernize China, the architect also had a share in two eminent conservation projects, the Palace Museum in Beijing and the restoration of the colonial town of Williamsburg (Virginia).

*

* *

Before early photography of China becomes a reliable historical source, there is much to do. By bringing out names and images never seen or written about before, and putting them back in their particular context, the present work may, at a modest level, have contributed to this sizeable task.

APPENDIX 1

GLOSSARY

Pinyin	*Traditional*	*Chinese*
European Palaces:		
Xieqiqu	Hsieh Ch'i Ch'ü	諧奇趣
Xushuilou	Hsü Shui Lou	蓄水樓
Yangquelong	Yang Ch'üeh Lung	養雀籠
Wanhuazhen Huayuan	Wan Hua Chen Hua Yüan	萬花陣花園
Fangwaiguan	Fang Wai Kuan	方外觀
Zhuting	Chu T'ing	竹亭
Haiyantang	Hai Yen T'ang	海晏堂
Guanshuifa	Kuan Shui Fa	觀水法
Dashuifa	Ta Shui Fa	大水法
Yuanyingguan	Yuan Ying Kuan	遠瀛觀
Xianfashanmen	Hsien Fa Shan Men	線法山門
Xianfashan	Hsien Fa Shan	線法山
Xianfashan Dongmen	Hsien Fa Shan Tung Men	線法山東門
Hudong Xianfahua	Hu Tung Hsien Fa Hua	湖東線法畫

Pinyin	*Traditional*	*Chinese*
Geography:		
Xiamen	Amoy	廈門
Baliqiao	Palichiao	八里橋
Beihe	Peiho	北河
Beijing	Peking	北京
Beitang	Pehtang	北塘
Changchunyuan	Ch'ang Ch'un Yuan	暢春園
Dagu	Taku	大沽
Fujian	Fukian	福建
Fuzhou	Foochow	福州
Guangdong	Kwangtung	廣東
Guangxi	Kwangsi	廣西
Haidian	Haitien	海甸
Hatamen	Hata Men	哈大門
Jiaozhou	Kiaochow	膠州
Juyongguan	Tuyong Kwan	居墉關
Nanjing	Nanking	南京
Beihai	Pakhoi	北海
Qianmen	Ch'ien Men	前門
Qingdao	Tsingtau	青島
Shamian	Shamien	沙面
Shandong	Shantung	山東
Tianjin	Tientsin	天津
Tianningsi	Tien Ling Sse	天寧寺
Tongzhou	Tungchow	通州
Wanshoushan	Wan Shou Shan	萬壽山
Xinjiang	Chinese Turkestan	新疆
Xiyanglou	Hsi Yang Lou	西洋樓

Pinyin	*Traditional*	*Chinese*
Yangzi jiang	Yangtze Kiang	揚子江
Yiheyuan	I-ho Yüan	頤和園
Yuanmingyuan	Yüan-ming-yüan	圓明園
Zhili	Chihli	直隸
People		
Cixi	Tz'u Hsi	慈禧
Hongzhan	Hong Chan	弘瞻
Jin Xun	Chin Hsün	金勳
Kangxi	K'ang Hsi	康熙
Lei (family)	Lei	雷
Qianlong	Ch'ien Lung	乾隆
Tongzhi	T'ung Chih	同治
Xianfeng	Hsien Feng	咸豐
Xiangfei	Hsiang-fei	香妃
Xuantong	Hsuan T'ung	宣統
Yongzheng	Yung Cheng	雍正
Yongle	Yung Lo	永樂
Other		
haiguan	hai kuan	海關
pailou	p'ai lou	牌樓
Qing	Ch'ing	清
Qinghua College	Tsing Hua College	清華大學
Taiping	Taiping	太平
Tongwenguan	T'ung-wen kuan	同文館
Zongli yamen	Tsungli Yamen	總理衙門

APPENDIX 2

CHRONOLOGY

Influential Events in China		Other	
1842	Treaty of Nanjing, 5 ports open to international trade	1821–50	Daogan Emperor
1850–64	Taiping Rebellion	1851–61	Xianfeng Emperor
1858	Canton seized by British troops; Treaty of Tianjin		
1859	Franco-British assault on Dagu forts repulsed		
1860	Franco-British Campaign; Rape of the Summer Palace; Beijing seized; Treaty of Beijing; 10 new ports open; Western residence in Beijing allowed	*October 1860*	*First photographs of Beijing: Fauchery, Beato*
1861	Regency of Dowager Empress Cixi	1861–75	Tongzhi Emperor
		c. 1867	*Ohlmer shipwrecked on the China coast*
1870	Massacre of missionaries in Tianjin	*1870*	*Thomas Child arrives in Beijing* *Théophile Piry arrives in China*
1873	Emperor's majority and wedding		
1875	Regency of Dowager Empress Cixi	1875–1908	Guangxu Emperor
1884–5	Sino-French war		
		1889	*Thomas Child leaves China*
1894–95	Sino-Japanese war		
1896	Manchuria under Russian control		
1897–99	China "carved out" among foreign nations		
1900	Boxer Rebellion; Siege of the Beijing legations	*1900*	*Mumm von Schwarzenstein arrives in Beijing*
1901	Treaties between China and foreign nations		

		1903	*Sophus Black arrives in Beijing*
		1906	*Mumm von Schwarzenstein appointed to Japan*
1908	Death of Dowager Empress Cixi	1908–11	Xuantong Emperor (Puyi)
1911	Chinese Revolution		
1912	Abdication of Emperor		
		1914	*Ernst Ohlmer leaves China*
		1914–18	First World War
		1915–18	*C.W. Bishop's first mission in China*
1916	Warlord Period starts	*1916*	*Théophile Piry leaves China*
		1919	*Conrad Anner arrives in Beijing*
1921	Foundation of the Chinese Communist Party		
		1922	*Osvald Sirén in Beijing*
		1923–27	*C.W. Bishop's second mission in China*
1924	Definition of nationalist-communist cooperation		
1925	Death of Sun Wen (Sun Yat Sen)		
1927	Break between nationalits and communists; Jiang Jieshi (Chiang Kai-chek)'s troops seize Beijing		
		1930	*Conrad Anner leaves China*
1931	Occupation of Manchuria by Japan	*1931*	*Sophus Black leaves China*
1931–35	Japan expands in North China		
1934–35	The Long March	*1934*	*C.W. Bishop leaves China*

APPENDIX 3
THE EUROPEAN PALACES OF THE YUANMINGYUAN: RESEARCH AND PHOTOGRAPHY

THE MISSION PALAIS D'ÉTÉ

As there is no single detailed contemporary source on the subject, at present researching the European Palaces is a difficult task. If the site is clearly identified and still exists as such, the original design of the garden has been almost entirely destroyed. No area can be recreated from the sparse remains and restoration of the original state is simply out of the question. In addition, any comprehensive study involves, at least, the fields of architecture, the history of Western art, the history of Chinese art, the history of landscaping (Chinese and Western) and botany. Failing a Renaissance scholar with universal knowledge, this had to be the work of a team, and this is why the Mission Palais d'Eté was created in Paris in 1983 to conduct research on the European Palaces.

Headed by Michèle Pirazzoli-t'Serstevens, the Mission was for several years sponsored by the French Ministry of Foreign Affairs. Work has involved general and detailed mapping and plotting of the site, paper reconstruction, study and identification of planting, as well as retracing the history of the garden from its conception and construction to the stages of its destruction. The members' publications and communications cover the timing and circumstances of the erection of the palaces and the use of the buildings based on eighteenth century Chinese and Western sources (Michèle Pirazzoli-t'Serstevens); the study of relief and perspective; the creation of maps and of a scale model of the site and paper reconstructions of several facades and ground areas (Antoine Durand); studies of plants and landscaping (Marie-Pierre Dumoulin-Genest and Gilles Genest); determination of the Western sources used by the Jesuits (Vincent Droguet); documentation of these same Western sources (Andrée Bureau); and the collection, inventory and study of old photographic and other nineteenth and twentieth century documents and of the process of destruction (Régine Thiriez).

The on-site work had to be limited to measuring spare components and surveying the current lay of the land. The Mission's two surveys took place before the latest reconstructions; they would now be impossible. Ultimately, the major sources for filling in the gaps are archives.

PRIMARY SOURCES ON THE EUROPEAN PALACES

Chinese sources include the official archives of the Qing dynasty, which are gradually being published. The relevant documents available deal with the Yuanmingyuan proper as well as with financial or political matters.

No blueprints or maps drawn by the Jesuit builders have come to light. They may still be hidden in some Chinese repository, but it is more likely that such documents were kept at the Yuanmingyuan and destroyed in the 1860 fire. It is possible, however, that the Jesuits sent to Europe sketches which have yet to be found.[1] The search is all the more difficult because the Jesuit order was dissolved shortly after the construction of the European Palaces, while subsequent wars and revolutions affected archives in several relevant countries, most notably France. Likewise, no nineteenth century architect set himself the task of surveying the site when it was still close to its original condition. Only a small map of the site dated 1873 and drawn by an unknown author (maybe Ernst Ohlmer), shows that someone attempted to do early amateur research (see Teng Gu 1933).

Maps in the Chinese mode survive. Some were previously in the archives of the Lei family, architects of the Yuanmingyuan for several generations. They were inserted into Adam's *Yuen Ming Yuen* (1926) by Chin Hsün (Jin Xun) from the National Library, who also added some of his own sketches.[2] However, these documents can only be used to supplement sources such as modern surveys.

There are secondary sources to substitute for the archives unavailable to us. Few focus exclusively on the European Palaces. The schedule of construction and the builders involved are discussed here and there in Jesuit letters to Europe. There are also a few first-hand accounts of visits to the European Palaces in the nineteenth century. French and British military archives on the 1860 Rape of the Summer Palace contain no useful material on the garden. Likewise, uncovered descriptions are too general and sketchy to be useful. However, there are a few exceptions, such as the French diplomat who drew a precise sketch of the facade of the Belvedere in the 1860s and mentioned its "purple and green tiled roof" ([Devéria] 1876:2, 230). Regrettably, few nineteenth and twentieth century missionaries showed any interest in this rare example of eighteenth century Jesuit secular architectural work in China.

At strict iconographical level, there are two types of sources. The best known is a suite of twenty engravings commissioned in 1783 by the Qianlong emperor and showing the major sites (buildings and landscapes) of the garden.[3] The second source is photography.

PHOTOGRAPHING THE EUROPEAN PALACES

The information provided by the photographs takes many forms. Each image is a step, large or small, showing its full value only when integrated into the whole collection. Haphazard as the one hundred fifty-odd photographs may appear from the previous pages, they provide a quantity of precious information not available either from archives or the remaining ruins.

For the researchers of the Mission Palais d'Eté, their input took several essential shapes. The concrete and reliable evidence on appearance, volumes and proportions of the buildings was essential for the architects reconstructing the original site. They could also properly place scattered fragments, identify the methods of construction not clear from the ruins, the nature of the building material, the original configuration of the landscape, and get the general layout and some of the key planting. Likewise, the art historians found the early photographs a useful support to recreate volumes while visiting the site. They also relied extensively on the images in their search for the builders' original sources of inspiration, whether global or of details, and for stylistic studies. The landscape architect found in the collection an important source on the species and their particular treatment (trimming, etc.), and of the use of vegetals in the composition of volume, space and visual transitions.

The early photographs by Ohlmer, Piry and Child, and from Uslar and Durham, are references on the state of the garden shortly after the 1860 fire. All of the series provide important views, and there is surprisingly little overlap in their coverage of the site. Besides their real quality, they are the only photographic record of a number of vistas soon to be irreversibly altered or destroyed. The coverage of the Xieqiqu is especially thorough, and even some species of trees around the Haiyantang and the Belvedere are recognizable.

In addition to showing the buildings as close to their original state as they are ever likely to be found, the superior definition of both wet collodion plates and albumen prints allows excellent enlargements of small details significant for the history of the palaces and their architecture. Only photography could reveal the intricacy of the decoration, this extraordinary blend of Chinese and Western traditions, of marble and brick, of ceramic and stone. Because of the long exposure time and whatever the distance between them, the background is as clear as the main subject. Discoveries are endless: a truly astonishing one was that the originally plastered bricks of the bearing wall of the north terrace of the Xieqiqu were laid horizontally on one side and following the stairs slant on the other. Was the palace built so fast that two different teams worked on either side of the stairs, one of them misunderstanding the blueprints?

An unexpected benefit of the research was the revelation of the process of destruction of the European Palaces between 1873 and 1925, and of its rate of progress.

This is the mute but eloquent chronicle of a slow eradication. The nineteenth century views all prove that the palaces withstood the 1860 fire relatively well. Traces of the blaze are clear in the prints, with the almost complete collapse of the roofs and the scorched stone and marble surrounding the openings. However, the rest of the facades still appear strong and in good condition, especially the glazed ceramic tiles which had been fired in kilns and were thus able to withstand extreme heat.

The actual disappearance of the buildings was due to neglect, pilfering or simple vandalism. Thus, by 1876, all the marble balustrades of the Xieqiqu stairs had been thrown to the ground; this was also when the marble and glazed ceramic crown moldings of the Dashuifa and the Yuanyingguan were torn off.

Curiously, other parts remained. Although easy to carry, the fountain-vases in the Aviary recesses were still *in situ* when the structure was finally dismantled around 1924. Here as elsewhere, the motive for the destruction was the recovery of the bricks, a modest building material essential in north China. Stone and marble were apparently less desirable, probably because they had been cut into Western shapes and designs hard to incorporate into Chinese architecture. However, it is known that quantities of Yuanmingyuan marble were burned to make lime.

The images follow the site's degradation after 1860 and explain the process. The palace most photographed in the nineteenth century, the Xieqiqu, was built with small-sized building material which made it especially vulnerable. In 1901, it had already been reduced to a pile of rubble unattractive to photographers. Conversely, the Yuanyingguan and the Haiyantang were shown more and more with the passage of time.

Without photography, our perception of the European Palaces would be sketchy at best. However, the sum of the images is far from covering the whole garden. A major failing is the absence of early panoramas; presumably, the visual obstacles between the small "landscapes" devised by the Jesuits were still too effective for them to be done (for example, trees prevented the westward exposures from the top of the Haiyantang which could be done later.)

In 1901, Mumm gave a limited but important update at the end of a crucial period of blackout that lasted until the turn of the century. Later, Alimoff, Anner, Bishop, Black and Sirén considerably tightened the site coverage, whether through distant shots defining the landscape (Bishop, Black), or through views or close ups of the ruins which reveal the methods of construction (all). The general integration of the palaces within the garden walls was made clear, as was the ornamentation on these walls which the 1783 engravings had severely distorted.

At architectural level, the twentieth century group of views is much more than a simple extension of the nineteenth century portfolio. Crucial contributions are the coverage of zones or angles previously unseen and the display of construction methods. In this theatrical architecture, coatings and facings had disguised the inner structure, revealed only when it was bared. This is where the brick core appears, where the facings show their profile and the imprint of the mortises attaching them to walls, where the very nature of the decoration becomes clear: while coating crumbles, marble breaks and flimsy walls are betrayed by holes.

Nevertheless, there is still room for new discoveries to provide essential information on the site, especially for the early years. The 1994 simultaneous discovery, after years of research, in Uslar (Germany) and Durham (England), of prints showing entirely new early views, could be repeated. On the other hand, gaps are likely to remain; due to lack of space or early damage, some perspectives were closed for as long as the structure stood.

*
* *

Because of this, and because it came after the fire, it cannot be claimed that photography can replace the on-site surveys or even the 1783 engravings in studies of the European Palaces. It is, however, an essential complement to them.

Considering the diverse and sometimes conflicting needs, it is also difficult to claim that one photographer is more important than another. If the inner structure of a facade seen and photographed in 1877 is explained by an 1915 view, which image is the most important? This is for the researcher to decide, depending on whether decoration or construction techniques are the object of the study.

A personal choice is that the older the photographs, the more interesting they are, because they are closer to the original state. There is also their quality as monumental photographs, their clarity and unique closeness, their handcrafted nature. One can "walk" into an early photograph of the Xieqiqu—also an essential quality of Chinese painted landscape. Of the more recent photographs, however, the picnic and the threshing scenes by Piry (Fig. 50, 51) are a precious intrusion of real life in a fantasy world.

Finally, the grouping of photographs also shows that, just as the European Palaces have become identified in many minds with the Yuanmingyuan, the architectural group formed by the Dashuifa and the Yuanyingguan had, by the twentieth century, become the representative image of the European Palaces. To this day, this makes it that of the Yuanmingyuan.

APPENDIX 4

PAUL CHAMPION

Photographs made in China and Japan, 1865–66

Description	1	2	3	4	5	Other
Self-portrait in Chinese Dress	—	006702	—	—	—	—
Beijing						
Musicians	57276	006707	4303	2:225	—	7
Palanquin carried	57277	—	4295	1:326	—	—
Palanquin on ground	57278	—	4295bis	—	—	—
Old man in winter costume	57275	006708	4292	1:315	—	7(alt'd)
Cobbler	—	006712	—	—	—	
Beggars' Bridge	57269	006703	64–7866	2:197	—	9:232 10:281 11:287
Hatamen Street	57270	006704	—	1:335	—	9:232
Qianmen	57272	006710	7868	1:332	fig.6	—
Market near Qianmen	57268	006714	—	—	—	SFP
Outside along the Walls	57274	006716	—	1:329	—	—
Temple of Heaven	57273	006717	—	—	fig.7	SFP
Pailou	57271	006706	7860	—	fig.8	9
Chinese house	—	—	—	—	fig.5	—
Square kiosk in mosque	—	006711	—	2:239	—	—
Temple in Wanshoushan	—	006713	—	2:221	—	—
Porcelain tower at Wanshoushan, with bells	—	006709	—	—	—	9:314 10:271
Pagoda Tongzhou	—	—	64–7874	2:229	fig.4	—
Old tower pagoda	—	006715	*not* 64–7872	2:223	—	—
Treaty Ports						
Tingdon pagoda near Shanghai	57279	—	—	—	—	—
Cotton weaving, Hankew	—	—	—	—	fig.3	—
Chinese junks, Hankew	—	006720	—	—	—	—
American consulate Hankew	57280	—	—	—	—	—
Hankou, Confluent of Yangzi River	—	—	—	—	—	8 9:401

Description	1	2	3	4	5	Other
Woman of Ningbo	—	—	—	—	—	SFP
Man in Ningbo	—	—	—	—	—	SFP
Tomb in Ningbo	—	006719	—	—	—	—
Group of people near tomb	—	006718	—	—	—	—
Japan						
Palanquin of Nagasaki	57285	006705	—	—	fig.1	—
Musicians of Nagasaki	57284	006721	—	—	—	—
Japanese workers (Nagasaki)	—	—	—	—	fig.2	—
View Nagasaki (1)	57287	—	—	—	—	—
View Nagasaki (2)	57286	—	—	—	—	—
View Yokohama	57283	—	—	—	—	—
Total	18	20	8	11	8	11

Champion used 27 × 33cm plates during his trip ("*Remarques sur les difficultés que présente la Photographie dans les contrées telles que la Chine et le Japon*", *BSFP* 1867, 13–18.)

1. Victoria & Albert Museum Photographic Collection, London: unsigned, original prints, very homogeneous as to size and presentation.
2. Musée d'Orsay, Paris: original prints, some signed, all with dry stamp "PC".
3. Morache Collection at Musée de l'Homme, Paris: copyprints, reduced size, marked Morache; no records; complete numbers are "43-[above number]-173".
4. G. Devéria [*alias* Choutzé], "Pékin et le nord de la Chine", *Le Tour du Monde* 1876: att. Morache.
5. P. Champion, "La Chine et le Japon", *Etudes sur l'Exposition de 1867. Annales et archives de l'industrie au XIXème siècle . . .* , Eugène Lacroix, Paris, 1869; att. "author".
6. Société Française de Photographie, Paris (SFP): recorded as gifts (1867); dry stamp "PC".
7. *L'Illustration*, 13 September 1873: att. Paul Champion.
8. J. von Hübner, *Promenade autour du Monde*, Hachette, Paris, 1877; attr. "author".
9. E. Reclus, *Nouvelle Géographie Universelle*, v. VII, *Asie Orientale*. Hachette, Paris, 1882: att. Paul Champion.
10. *Capitales du Monde*, Hachette, Paris, 1896 att. Champion.
11. R. Cortambert, *Voyage pittoresque à travers le monde*, 4th ed., Hachette, Paris, 1884.

APPENDIX 5

TABLE OF PHOTOGRAPHS

The following tables present the photographs of the European Palaces identified for the period. Photographers are listed in alphabetical order, and the views follow the normal sequence of visit.

Information includes:

- a reference, combining the photographer's name and a specific number (see each table for details);
- a short description;
- significant characteristics and additional copies; technical qualities are appreciated for the most significant source only (i.e., negative preferred to print, print to photoengraving, etc.);
- the apparent date of the photograph;
- reference to comparable images in the study; whenever the buildings altered significantly between photographs, the latter are cross-referenced;
- an appreciation of the importance of the photograph as a source on the European Palaces, in connection with the whole collection: when several similar views exist, all lose importance as each one is easily replaced. The marks go from "A" (essential source), to "B" (only photograph of building/angle), "C" (only photograph at that stage), and "D" (significant image).

ALIMOFF[1]

Reference[2]	Description	Charac-teristics	Apparent Date	Relate to	Importance
Alimoff 22	Xieqiqu, south. Central wing		1922	Sirén a Anner 20R-T Bishop 728–79	D–Structure of east bearing wall and of base
Alimoff 23	Xieqiqu, south. Marble shell on ground		1922		
Alimoff 21	Xushuilou, SW. Through Xieqiqu north pilasters		1922	Bishop 728–10 Anner/Other 3	B–New angle; places Xieqiqu and Xushuilou
Alimoff 24	Haiyantang, west. Fountain		1922		
Alimoff 17	Dashuifa and Yuanyingguan, south		1922	Anner 20R-B Sirén d Black 3377	
Alimoff 20	Dashuifa, SE. Arch and east pillar		1922		
Alimoff 18	Yuanyingguan, south. Left ornate column	inscribed on back "photo printed in August of 1922"	1922	Anner 82-B Black 3379 Sirén Pal-215	
Alimoff 19	Yuanyingguan, SE. Left ornate column		1922	Anner 82-B Black 3379 Sirén Pal-215	B–For wall behind column

[1] First name was not recorded

[2] Reference numbers are the end part of numbers in Photographic Collection of Musée National des Arts Asiatiques Guimet: full reference is 6 A 1437/17 to 24

CONRAD W. ANNER

Reference[1]	Description	Charac-teristics	Apparent Date	Relate to	Importance
Anner/Other 1[2]	The European Palaces, westward from the Chinese garden	UC/VUA[3] *OBP 248*[4]	c. 1911–12		A–With Bishop 728–18, only panorama from outside the enclosure. Informative on layout of both Chinese and European enclosures
Anner 20-T	Xieqiqu and Lake, SE, with Xushuilou, Maze and back pavilion	wide; *OBP 245*	c. 1911–12	Black 3366 Misc. 1	B–Last photograph of Xieqiqu as a coherent whole
Anner 20-M	Xieqiqu, SE, with Gate to Maze and back pavilion. Wall in forefront	wide; n° 552[5]	c. 1911–12	Mumm 182 Bishop 728-27 Misc. 2	B–Layout
Anner 20R-T	Xieqiqu, south. Central wing	wide; n° 543	c. 1911–12	Sirén a, Pal-207 Alimoff 22	
Anner 63R-ML	Xieqiqu, south. East pavilion	small	c. 1911–12?	Sirén b Anner/Other 2	
Anner/Other 2	Xieqiqu, south. East pavilion	*OBP 246*	c. 1911–12	Anner 63R-ML	
Anner 63R-TR	Downward from top of Xieqiqu, south. Basin, pavement, pavilion and Chinese garden	small	c. 1911–12?		A–Only bird's eye view study; detailed layout
Anner 61-TL	Xieqiqu, south. Columns, eastward	small	c. 1911–12		
Anner 20-B	Xieqiqu, west	wide; n° 541 *OBP 240*	c. 1911–12		D–Only view of central wing from west
Anner 63R-BR	Xieqiqu, east. North gallery and terrace	small	c. 1911–12?		

Reference[1]	Description	Charac-teristics	Apparent Date	Relate to	Importance
Anner/Other 3	Xieqiqu, east. North terrace, Xushuilou	*Schulz[7] pl. 11*	c. 1911–12	Black 3367 Alimoff 21	B
Anner 80-T	Xieqiqu, north	wide; graffiti (text)	c. 1911–12	Ohlmer 6 Child 198 Bishop 728–19	A–Shell of north gallery, stairs
Anner 81-M	Xushuilou, NW, with partition wall	wide; n° 556	c. 1911–12	Anner 81R-M	B–From outside enclosure
Anner 81R-M	Xushuilou, NW	also glass slide n° 249; wide; n° 553[5]; *Schulz pl. 12; OBP 239*	c. 1911–12	Anner 81-M	B–From outside enclosure
Anner 82R-B	Gate to Aviary	wide	c. 1911–12	Bishop 728–1/2/7 Black 3368 Sirén Pal-213	
Anner 63B-L	Belvedere, east. With bridge, Haiyantang	small	c. 1911–12?	Piry 3	
Anner 82R-M	Belvedere, SE	wide; n° 539; *OBP 244*	c. 1911–12		
Anner 82R-T	Belvedere, south. Center	wide; n° 536	c. 1911–12		
Anner 63R-TL	Westward from Haiyantang. Xushuilou and Xieqiqu, hills on left	small; panorama	c. 1911–12?		D
Anner 63R-BL	Westward from Haiyantang. Belvedere, Gate to Aviary, Xushuilou and Xieqiqu	small; panorama	c. 1911–12?	Piry 4 Black 3374 Bishop 728–16	D–Places buildings

Reference[1]	Description	Charac-teristics	Apparent Date	Relate to	Importance
Anner 63-BR	Haiyantang, west. Ornate marble base and fountain	small	c. 1911–12?	Black 3372	D–People above shell give scale
Anner 20R-M	Haiyantang, west. Fountain and reservoir, NW	wide; n° 546	c. 1911–12		D–Profile of fountain, ramps, structure of west wing with turret
Anner/Other 4	Haiyantang, westward. Fountain with curved staircase, west wing and reservoir	wide; *Perzynski*[8] *pl. 7 bottom*	c. 1911–12		B–Links wings; as west wing is ruined, details of base are revealed
Anner 81R-T	Haiyantang, NW. Reservoir	wide; n° 559; *Schulz pl. 32*	c. 1911–12		D
Anner 81-B	Haiyantang, SE. Reservoir	wide; n° 558; *Schulz pl. 33; OBP 238*	c. 1911–12	Piry 6 Misc. 4	D
Anner 246	Throne, north	glass slide only; *OBP 247*	c. 1911–12	Piry 8 Black 3376	
Anner 248	Dashuifa, south	glass slide only	c. 1911–12		
Anner 20R-B	Dashuifa and Yuanyingguan, south	wide	c. 1911–12	Black 3377 Alimoff 17	B–Shows basin and space left of Yuanyingguan
Anner 82-M	Dashuifa and Yuanyingguan, SW	wide	c. 1911–12	Bishop 728–17	
Anner 82-T	Dashuifa and Yuanyingguan, south	wide; *OBP 243*	c. 1911–12	Sirén d, Pal-215	
Anner 82-B	Yuanyingguan, south. Left ornate column and two openings	also glass slide n° 247; wide; *Perzynski pl. 7 top; OBP 237*	c. 1911–12	Piry 10 Black 3379 Sirén Pal-215 Alimoff 18, 19	D–Ornaments and inside structure

Reference[1]	Description	Charac-teristics	Apparent Date	Relate to	Importance
Anner 81-T	Yuanyingguan, NW. Corner	wide	c. 1911–12	Bishop 728–9	A–Only view of north facade
Anner 81R-B	Yuanyingguan, west. Left.	wide	c. 1911–12	Sirén f	D

[1] Author's reference numbers. Most send back to the Rockefeller Archive Center (RAC) Anner collection. They are made of (i) the number appearing on the sheet bearing the print, with "**R**" for reverse side"; (ii) the location of the print (**T**op, **M**iddle, **B**ottom, and, if relevant, "**R**ight" or "**L**eft".)

[2] "Anner/Other" numbers refer to prints not in the Anner collection, but belonging to the same series.

[3] Print in United Church/Victoria University Archives, Toronto, series "Peking, China. Imperial Palace. Old Summer Palace".

[4] "OBP" refers to Fu Gongyue, *Old Beijing in Panorama* (1992), with the plate number. This work presents ten images of the European Palaces, apparently taken from the same numbered series (see p. 109.) However, the date given for the prints, "1860", is clearly erroneous.

[5] Number on print (from negative.)

[6] Smaller size prints, possibly later, for which no satisfactory cross-referencing could be done.

[7] Schulz, Alexander, *Hsi Yang Lou: Untersuchungen zu den "Europaische Bauten" des Kaiser Ch'ien-lung*, Würzburg Universität, 1966.

[8] Perzynski, Friedrich, *Von Chinas Göttern: Reisen in China*, München: Kurt Wolff Verlag, 1920.

CARL WHITING BISHOP

Reference[1]	Description	Charac-teristics	Apparent Date	Relate to	Importance
Bishop 728–18	Southward from Chinese garden, European Palaces wall, with top of Haiyantang	panorama	c. 1923–25		With Anner/Other 1, only panorama from Chinese garden. Not otherwise significant
Bishop 728–27	Xieqiqu, SE. East pavilion and wall		1915	Anner 20-M	
Bishop 728–79	Xieqiqu, south. Detail of central wing		1915	Alimoff 22	
Bishop 728–15	Xieqiqu, child standing among ruins		c. 1923–25		
Bishop 728–3	Xieqiqu, south. West pavilion and gallery		1915	Anner 20-M Bishop 728–8	
Bishop 728–8	Xieqiqu, south. West gallery and wall		1915	Bishop 728–3	
Bishop 728–11	Xieqiqu, child near a marble shell		c. 1923–25		
Bishop 728–19	Xieqiqu, north, with west gallery	graffiti (text)	c. 1923–25	after Anner-80-T	D–Only global view of a gallery from the north (see Ohlmer 5 for partial view)
Bishop 728–10	Xushuilou, east		1915	before Sirén-Pal-211 Alimoff 21	A
Bishop 728–13	Maze, south. With base of central kiosk, back pavilion and space beyond		c. 1923–25		A–Only view of maze with layout
Bishop 728–7	Gate to Aviary, front		1915	Anner 82 R-B Black 3372 Sirén Pal-213	D–With right wall
Bishop 728–1	Gate to Aviary, front		1915	see above	D–Well contrasted
Bishop 728–2	Gate to Aviary, SE		1915	see above	

Reference[1]	Description	Characteristics	Apparent Date	Relate to	Importance
Bishop 728–21	Belvedere, west. Bridge and part of Haiyantang		c. 1923–25		D–Bridge
Bishop 728–14	Belvedere, west. Child in front of bridge		c. 1923–25		D–Shallowness of river bed
Bishop 728–6	Belvedere, SE		1915	before Black-3370/3371	D–Structure
Bishop 728–4	Westward from Haiyantang. North wall, Belvedere, Gate to Aviary	panorama; cultivation	1915	before Bishop 728–16	
Bishop 728–16	Westward from Haiyantang. Belvedere, Gate to Aviary, Xushuilou, Xieqiqu	panorama; cultivation	c. 1923–25	after Bishop 728–4 Anner 63R-BL Piry 4 Black 3374	D
Bishop 728–20	Haiyantang, west. Ornate marble base, south wall and hill		c. 1923–25		D–Respective height of wall and hill
Bishop 728–5	Haiyantang, west. Fountain		1915		D
Bishop 728–23	Haiyantang, west. Fountain, southward		c. 1923–25		D–Elements of fountain, mostly on ramps
Bishop 728–22	Haiyantang. Pilaster		c. 1923–25		
Bishop 728–9	Eastward from Haiyantang. Yuanyingguan and Dashuifa.	panorama; cultivation	1915	Anner 81R-T Bishop 728–12 Sirén f	A–Only whole view of Yuanyingguan; layout with Dashuifa, wall
Bishop 728–12	Eastward from Haiyantang. Yuanyingguan and Dashuifa	panorama; cultivation	c. 1923–25	Piry 7 Bishop 728–12 Sirén f	D–inferior to 728–9, it shows changes over 8–10 years
Bishop 728–17	Dashuifa and Yuanyingguan, SW		c. 1923–25	after Anner 82-T	
Bishop 391–8	Two children and a sculpted element on the ground		c. 1923–25	same children as Bishop 728–11/14/15	

[1] Photographer's reference numbers, as used by the Freer Gallery of Art/Arthur M. Sackler Gallery.

SOPHUS BLACK

Reference[1]	Description	Characteristics	Apparent Date	Relate to	Importance
Black 3366	Xieqiqu, SW. With reservoir and back pavilion beyond maze		c. 1915–18	Misc. 1 Anner 20-T	D
Black 3367	Xieqiqu, north. Westward, stairs, terrace and Xushuilou		c. 1915–18	Anner-Other 3	D
Black 3368	Gate to Aviary	graffiti (characters and numbers) on vertical slabs	c. 1915–18	Anner 82R-B Bishop 728–1/2/7 Sirén Pal-213	
Black 3369	Haiyantang, west. From Aviary gate		c. 1915-18	Sirén Pal-208	D
Black 3370	Belvedere, south. Center right (no stairs)	graffiti (oculus parts numbered: 142, 143, etc.; text on left)	c. 1915–18	Bishop 728–6	D–For structure
Black 3371	Belvedere, SW. Whole with bridge		c. 1915–18	Bishop 728–6 Sirén Pal-212	D
Black 3372	Haiyantang, west. Ornate marble base		c. 1915-18	Anner 63-BR	
Black 3373	Haiyantang, west. Fountain with shell and south part, slanted	graffiti on shell, "212"	c. 1915–18	Gamble-244–1372 Sirén Pal-209	D
Black 3374	Westward and downward from Haiyantang. Belvedere, site of Bamboo Gazebos, Gate to Aviary, south wall		c. 1915–18	Anner 63R-BL Piry 4 Bishop 728–16	B–Places Bamboo Gazebos

Reference[1]	Description	Charac-teristics	Apparent Date	Relate to	Importance
Black 3375	Ceramic decoration embedded in wall		c. 1915-18		B
Black 3376	Throne	graffiti (slabs between trophies numbered "204" to "207")	c. 1915–18	Anner 246 Piry 8	
Black 3377	Dashuifa and Yuanyingguan, south. From right of the Throne	blurred	c. 1915–18	Anner 20R-B Alimoff 17	
Black 3378	Dashuifa, SW, upward		c. 1915–18		
Black 3379	Yuanyingguan, south. Left ornate column with half opening on either side		c. 1915–18	Anner 82-B Sirén Pal-215 Alimoff 18,19	D–Shows tie-rods between cornice and wall
Black 3380	Yuanyingguan, south. Broken right ornate column, on the ground		c. 1915–18		
Black 3381	Yuanyingguan. Carved block on the ground	c. 1915–18			
Black 3382	Yuanyingguan, east. Central niche		c. 1915-18	Sirén e	D–Detail of sculpture, masonry; non-bearing wall is only one-brick thick
Black 3383	Yuanyingguan, east		c. 1915–18	Sirén e	B–See comment to 3382
Black 3384	Westward from Hill of Perspective. Gate, Yuanyingguan, Dashuifa, Throne, Haiyantang, partition and outside walls	panorama; cultivation; blurred	c. 1915–18		A
Black 3385	Gate and Hill of Perspective, east	cultivation	c. 1915–18		A

[1] Reference numbers from the Department of Ethnology of the National Museum, Copenhagen, Denmark.

THOMAS CHILD

Reference[1]	Description	Charac-teristics	Apparent Date	Relate to	Importance
Child 202	Xieqiqu, south. East pavilion and central wing	signed	1877	Ohlmer 1, 3 Piry 1 *Next state is Mumm 182, c. 1901*	B–*Most of Child's views are superseded by Ohlmer's which show an earlier, more complete state of the palaces*
Child 201	Xieqiqu, south. Central wing	signed, dated	1877		B
Child 200	Xieqiqu, south. Central wing, SE		1877	Ohlmer 3	
Child unum.	Xieqiqu, south. Central wing with top lintel missing	signed, dated; *Favier ed. 1898 pl. XI top*	1878	Child 200 *Next state is Anner 20R-T, c. 1912*	A–Last 19th century view of the palace
Child 203	Xieqiqu, south. West pavilion and arch of gallery	signed, dated	1877	Uslar 2	
Child 199	Xieqiqu, east. Gallery, central wing, east pavilion	signed, dated	1877	Uslar 3 Ohlmer 5	D
Child 198	Xieqiqu, north. With fountain and four trees	signed, dated	1877	Ohlmer 6 *Next state is Anner 80-T, c. 1912*	D
Child 204	Gate to Aviary, east	signed, dated	1877	*Next state is Mumm 183, c. 1901*	A–Only view whole

Reference[1]	Description	Charac-teristics	Apparent Date	Relate to	Importance
Child 205	Haiyantang, west. Facade, center with fountain	signed, dated	1877	Ohlmer 11 *Next state is Anner 20R-M, c. 1912*	A–For fountain
Child 206	Eastern Princes Gate, north	signed, dated	1877		A–Only view, with Ohlmer 13, showing the layout
Child 207	Yuanyingguan, south. Center	(signed, dated)	1877	Child 208 Ohlmer 15 *Next states are Anner 82-B and 20R-B, c. 1912*	
Child 208	Yuanyingguan, south. Center, closer	signed, dated	1877	Child 207 Ohlmer 15	D

[1] Photographer's reference numbers

ORIENTAL MUSEUM–UNIVERSITY OF DURHAM

Reference[1]	Description	Characteristics	Apparent Date	Relate to	Importance
Durham 1	Xieqiqu, south. East pavilion, central basin, boundary hill, eastward	albumen print, 14x24.7 cm	1876	Ohlmer 4 Piry 1	A–Shows most of the basin and the background
Durham 2	Xieqiqu, north, upward from west	albumen print, round top corners, 15.5x24.3 cm	1876	See Ohlmer 6, Child 198	A–Very clear ornate base of stairs, and depth of north facade. Photographic study unusual in the European Palaces

[1] Author's reference numbers.

SIDNEY D. GAMBLE[1]

Reference[2]	Description	Charac-teristics	Apparent Date	Relate to	Importance
Gamble 72B780	Xieqiqu, south	celluloid rollfilm	c. 1923	Misc. 1	D
Gamble 244.1372	Belvedere, south	celluloid rollfilm graffiti (text)	c. 1923		D
Gamble	Haiyantang, west, wall to wall	celluloid rollfilm	c. 1923	Black 3372 Sirén Pal-209	D–Best encompassing view of this side; shows the striking detail of the two end walls standing over the ruins of the west wing and fountain. See Ohlmer 11 for 1873 state.
Gamble 72B782	Throne, north	celluloid rollfilm	c. 1920		D
Gamble 72B781	Dashuifa and Yuanyingguan, south from basin	celluloid rollfilm	c. 1920		
Gamble 72B783	Yuanyingguan, south (detail) with carved column	celluloid rollfilm	c. 1920		
Gamble 52B5631	Chinese pavilion leading to European Palaces	celluloid rollfilm	c. 1920	Sirén g	D

[1] Among over 4,000 indexed photographs in the Gamble Archive in New York (The Sidney D. Gamble Foundation for China Studies), are the seven views of the European Palaces listed above. Sidney D. Gamble (1890–1968) was a social scientist whose interest in the European Palaces cannot be documented. The photographs came to light in March 1997, when the whole study was completed. They did not bring any new information, but, in light of the importance of Gamble's work in China for the YMCA between 1917 and 1933, and of his influential published work, it appeared relevant to include the photographs in these pages.
[2] Gamble Archive reference numbers.

SIGNIFICANT SPARE IMAGES

Reference[1]	Description	Source	Apparent Date	Relate to	Importance
Misc. 1	Xieqiqu, south, with maze	H. von Perckhammer[2], *Peking*, 188	c. 1915	Mumm 182 Anner 20-T Black 3366 Gamble 72B780	A–Shot from top of wall. View includes ruins of the Xieqiqu and all significant landmarks beyond
Misc. 2	Outer wall by Xieqiqu	G. D. Musso, *La Cina ed i Cinesi*, 723	c. 1915	Anner 20-M	D
Misc. 3	Belvedere, south	By H. von Perckhammer, in *Atlantis* journal, February 1931, 90	c. 1915	Ohlmer 9 Sirén Pal-212	Whole palace
Misc. 4	Haiyantang, SE	G. D. Musso, *La Cina ed i Cinesi*, 723	c. 1915	Anner 81-B Piry 6	A–Whole reservoir

[1] Author's reference numbers.

[2] In the study, Heinz von Perckhammer is the only professional photographer in a modern sense. He contributed in Germany to a number of books on various subjects, and was the author of three photographic albums on China. The most original is undoubtedly *Eine Nachteit in China,* nude photographs of Chinese women—a rarity in 1928, but not his only venture in the field. *Von China und Chinesen* (1930) is a booklet of forgivable images of China, but *Peking. Das Gesicht einer Stadt* (1928) presents large and well printed views of Beijing and its people, done in the luminous German style of the time.

N.B. A short series not studied here was found in the Benjamin March papers, Freer Gallery of Art/Arthur M. Sackler Gallery, Washington DC. The five small prints are dated 1926 and are not significant. Other publications deserving mention are G. Combaz, "Les palais impériaux de la Chine" (using only images by Child and Mumm von Schwarzenstein) and F. Perzynski, as discussed in pp. 109–110 in connection with Anner.

ALFONS MUMM VON SCHWARZENSTEIN

Reference[1]	Description	Charac-teristics	Apparent Date	Relate to	Importance
Mumm 182	Xieqiqu, south		1901	Misc. 1 *Next state is Anner 20-M, c. 1912*	C–State in 1901. See Ohlmer 1 for 1873 state
Mumm 183	Gate to Aviary, east		1901	Child 204 *Next state is Anner 82R-B, c. 1912*	C–State in 1901. See Child 204 for 1877 state
Mumm 185	Haiyantang, SW. Gallery and reservoir with west pump building		1901	*Next state is Anner 81R-T, c. 1912*	A–State in 1901. Shows stair gallery linking west wing to reservoir. Extends to left of Sirén Pal-210. See Ohlmer 11 for 1873 state
Mumm 184	Dashuifa and Yuanyingguan, SW		1901	*Next state is Anner 20R-B, c. 1912*	C–State in 1901. See Ohlmer 14 for 1873 state

[1] The numbers refer to pages in the *Tagebuch in Bildern* [c. 1902]. Respective captions are: *"Yüan-ming-yüan, Der alte Sommerpalast, von der Verbündeten 1860 zerstört"* (182); *"Europäisches Thor in Yüanmingyüan"* (183), *"Mittelgebäude im europäischen Stil für die Wesseranlagen von Yüanmingyüan"* (185), and *"Hautgebaude im Renaissancestil"* (184).

ERNST OHLMER

Reference[1]	Description	Charac-teristics	Apparent Date	Relate to	Importance
Ohlmer 1	Xieqiqu, south. Across the lake	wet collodion plate 20.2x25.3 cm	1873	See Child 202, Ohlmer 3 Piry 1 *Next state is Anner 20-T, c. 1912*	A–*Besides being the earliest known photographs, in general all of Ohlmer's views are important because negative plates (for 12 of them) or good original prints (for all) are available for study*
Ohlmer 2	Xieqiqu, south. West pavilion and central wing	albumen print, cropped to 16.3x22.1 cm	1873	Piry 2	B -*For the Xieqiqu, only Ohlmer's views show the stair balustrades in place*
Ohlmer 3	Xieqiqu, south. Central wing, SE	wet collodion plate 20.2x25.3 cm	1873	Child 200, 202 Ohlmer 1 Piry 1	B
Ohlmer 4	Xieqiqu, south. East gallery and pavilion from central landing	wet collodion plate 20.2x25.3 cm	1873		A–For layout and ornaments on the landing. See Durham 1 for setup
Ohlmer 5	Xieqiqu, east. Gallery, central wing, east pavilion	wet collodion plate 20x24 cm	1873	Child 199 Uslar 2	A–Very good definition; best image for ornaments and traces of fire
Ohlmer 6	Xieqiqu, north. Whole, with fountain and four trees	wet collodion plate 20.2x25.5 cm	1873	Child 198	A

Reference[1]	Description	Charac-teristics	Apparent Date	Relate to	Importance
Ohlmer 7	Gate to the Maze, south. With central kiosk, four Western men	wet collodion plate 20.4x25.4 cm	1873		A–No other images of this gate exist
Ohlmer 8	Central kiosk of Maze, east	albumen print, oval image, cropped to 12.6x17.8 cm	1873	*Next state is Bishop 728–13, c. 1923*	A–Also on Ohlmer 7. Only close up view of this important kiosk and of its base
Ohlmer 9	Belvedere, south-west	albumen print, cropped to 17.5x23.2 cm	1873	*Next state is Piry 3, c. 1913*	B–Essential. Ohlmer 9 and 10 are the only views before 1913; they were shot when the palace was still virtually intact
Ohlmer 10	Belvedere, south-east. With right curved balustrade	wet collodion plate 20.4x25.4 cm	1873	*Next state is Anner 82R-M, c. 1912*	A–Sole view of balustrade. See comment to Ohlmer 9
Ohlmer 11	Haiyantang, west. Facade with fountain	wet collodion plate 20.3x25.5 cm	1873	Child 205	A–Wider coverage than Child 205
Ohlmer 12	Haiyantang, west. Right part with boundary wall	wet collodion plate 20.3x25.4 cm	1873		A–For Haiyantang, general layout, and tree species

Reference[1]	Description	Charac-teristics	Apparent Date	Relate to	Importance
Ohlmer 13	Throne, north. With western Princes Gate	wet collodion plate 20.3x25.4 cm	1873	*Next state is Piry 8, c. 1913*	A–Sole view with crowning of Throne; also layout
Ohlmer 14	Dashuifa, south. With Yuanyingguan	wet collodion plate, broken, 20.3x25.4 cm	1873	*Next state is Mumm 184, c. 1901*	A–Sole view with crowning of Dashuifa, including clusters of ceramic flowers; shows Dashuifa vis-à-vis Yuanyingguan
Ohlmer 15	Yuanyingguan, south. Center	wet collodion plate 20.3x25.4 cm	1873	Child 207, 208	A–With Ohlmer 14, sole view of crowning of Yuanyingguan, an essential decorative item.

[1] Author's reference numbers.

A. THEOPHILE PIRY

Reference[1]	Description	Charac-teristics	Apparent Date	Relate to	Importance
Piry 1	Xieqiqu, south-west	6 known copies; 18.6x24 cm in Uslar	1876	Child 200 Ohlmer 1, 2, 3 Durham 1	D–Includes edge of lake and whole east gallery
Piry 2	Xieqiqu, south. West pavilion	copyprint	1876	Ohlmer 2	
Piry 3	Belvedere, south-east, with bridge	cultivation; stereoscopic autochrome plate: 4.5x8.2 cm	1912–3	Anner 63R-L	*Autochromes have little definition. In general, this limits their documentary value*
Piry 4	Westward from Haiyantang. Belvedere, Gate to Aviary, Xieqiqu, walls	panorama; cultivation; stereo-scopic autochrome plate: 4.5x8.2 cm	1912–3	Anner 63R-BL Bishop 728–16 Black 3374	B–See comment to Piry 3. Shows well the connection with the north hills in the Chinese garden, as well as the Western Hills in the distance
Piry 5	Haiyantang, north. Picnic along the north side of the reservoir, with Belvedere	cultivation; stereo-scopic silver gelatin plate: 10.5x4.4 cm; three different versions with same people changing places (with a static camera)	1911		D–Gives the layout of the area, with reservoir, west wing of palace, outside wall and Belvedere; only real-life scene in Yuanmingyuan with Piry 6

Reference[1]	Description	Charac-teristics	Apparent Date	Relate to	Importance
Piry 6	Haiyantang, east. Threshing corn with donkey	stereoscopic auto-chrome plate: 4.5x8.2 cm	1912–3	Anner 81-B Misc. 4	D–See comment to Piry 3. Striking illustration of the fall from grace of an imperial garden
Piry 7	Eastward from Haiyantang. Yuanyingguan, Dashuifa, Hill of Perspective, walls	panorama; cultivation; stereoscopic auto-chrome plate: 4.5x8.2 cm	1912–3	Bishop 728–12	D–See comment to Piry 3. Only vertical slabs remain on top of the hill
Piry 8	Throne, north. Close up	stereoscopic autochrome plate: 4.5x8.2 cm	1912–3	Anner 246 Black 3376 Sirén Pal-216	See comment to Piry 3
Piry 9	Dashuifa, south west. With Yuanyingguan	stereoscopic autochrome plate: 4.5x8.2 cm	1912–3		See comment to Piry 3
Piry 10	Yuanyingguan, south. Center	stereoscopic autochrome plate: 4.5x8.2 cm	1912–3	Anner 82-B Sirén Pal-215	See comment to Piry 3

[1] Author's reference numbers

OSVALD SIREN

Reference[1]	Description	Charac-teristics	Apparent Date	Relate to	Importance
Sirén a	Xieqiqu, south. Central wing		1922	Alimoff 22 Anner 20R-T	C–Structure of building
Sirén Pal-207	Xieqiqu, south. Columns and pilasters across palace		1922	Anner 20R-T	B
Sirén b	Xieqiqu, south. East pavilion	graffiti (text)	1922	Anner 63R-ML	
Sirén Pal-211	Xushuilou, east		1922	after Bishop-728–10	B
Sirén Pal-213	Gate to Aviary, front	graffiti (text)	1922	Anner 82R-B Black 3368 Bishop-728–1/2/7	D–Left wall, Xushuilou through opening, pavement. Compare with Child 204
Sirén Pal-208	Haiyantang, west, from Aviary gate		1922	Black 3369	D–Pavement, ground between gate and Haiyantang
Sirén Pal-212	Belvedere and bridge, SW		1922	Misc. 3 Black 3371	B
Sirén Pal-209	Haiyantang, west. Fountain		1922	Black 3372 Gamble-244.1372	B
Sirén c	Haiyantang, NW. With fountain and south wall and hill		1922		A
Sirén Pal-210	Haiyantang, south. Reservoir		1922		A–Follows on Mumm 185

Reference[1]	Description	Charac-teristics	Apparent Date	Relate to	Importance
Sirén Pal-216	Throne, north		1922	Piry 8	D–See Ohlmer 13
Sirén d	Dashuifa and Yuanyingguan, south. From edge of basin		1922	Alimoff 17 Anner 82-T	
Sirén Pal-214	Dashuifa and Yuanyingguan, SE. With ramp		1922		A–Connects Dashuifa and Yuanyingguan
Sirén Pal-215	Dashuifa and Yuanyingguan, south. Central porch		1922	Piry 10 Black 3379 Alimoff 18, 19 Anner 82-T, 82-B	A–For east wall of west wing
Sirén e	Yuanyingguan, east. Central niche	Graffiti (large characters engraved in niche)	1922	Black 3382, 3383	D–Graffiti not visible on Black
Sirén f	Yuanyingguan, SW. Right angle		1922	Bishop-728–9/12 Anner 81R-B	D–Complements Anner
Sirén g	Chinese pavilion leading to the European Palaces		1922	Gamble 52B563	D

[1] Author's reference numbers. Those numbers starting with "Pal" are page numbers in *Palais de Pékin*. The lone letters are specific to this study; they refer to unindexed prints from the Sirén Papers in the Östasiatiska Museet in Stockholm.

STADTMUSEUM–USLAR

Reference[1]	Description	Charac-teristics	Apparent Date	Relate to	Importance
Uslar 1	Clock gate SW of Xieqiqu, with Chinese roof on other side. Balustrade	albumen print, round top corners, 15x24.8 cm. Inscribed on back "OHLMER"	1873–7		A–Sole existing photograph. Shows Chinese roof on west side of gate.
Uslar 2	Xieqiqu, south. East pavilion	albumen print with oval mask, 19.6x25.5 cm	1876	Child 303	
Uslar 3	Xieqiqu, east. Gallery, central wing, east pavilion	albumen print, round top corners, 15x24.8 cm. Inscribed on back "OHLMER"	1876	Child 199 Ohlmer 5	D–Only view encompassing the Xieqiqu from south-west to north
Uslar 4	Pavilion on Hill of Perspective	albumen print with oval mask 19.9x24.5 cm	1873–7		A–Sole existing photograph. Next state is Piry 7 (c. 1913), from a distance

[1] Author's reference numbers.
N.B. The prints are faded.

NOTES

CHAPTER 1

1. The only Westerners allowed to live in Beijing before 1860 belonged to a small Russian religious, diplomatic and scientific mission. They may have made photographs earlier, but so far none is credited to them. They could circulate between Tianjin and the Great Wall, and Wilkinson (1885) mentioned seeing Russian graffiti dated 1831 and 1850 on walls of the Dabeisi, in the Western Hills.
2. The Itier plates are now in the Musée National de la Photographie in Bièvres, France.
3. "Daguerreotype and Lithographic Printing Establishment, Wellington Terrace. Coloured or outline views made of Hong Kong or China Scenery . . . " (Worswick and Spence 1978, 134).
4. See list of photographs published by Negretti and Zambra and their detailed description (*PN* 11 November 1859, 110–2 and 18 November 1859, 124–6). Rossier was formally identified by A. Smith ([1859], 27). He visited other countries on this "roving commission to the East" (*PN* 4 November 1859, 99–100). Photographs of China credited to the same firm, but not on the list, were used by the *ILN* (12 January 1861, 44).
5. Although his signature appears on only a few prints, the setting identifies his work. All studios had carpets, which are often a good clue; outdoor scenes or landscapes are more difficult to credit.
6. For example, a view of three women prisoners in a single cangue has been dated 1908 (Worswick and Spence 1978, 61), a date still used by authors. The relevance of the scene varies in connection with Chinese culture, the photographer, or the collector, depending upon whether it is considered an authentic post-1900 street scene, or the early photographer's reconstruction it is. In fact, a very similar image of two men in the same place and the same position proves that the two scenes were set up, and quite certainly made before 1880. The Royal Ontario Museum has albumen copies of the two images. Both were also used for postcards at the turn of the century.
7. Shelfmark 6/1, Royal Engineers Library, Chatham, U.K. For his departure south, see Vetch 1901, 184 n. 1. For his images of the Campaign, see Falconer 1982.
8. Twenty-four stereoscopic negatives from the former collection of Ferrier and Soulier, acquired by Roger-Viollet in 1970 (the nineteen views of China offered in Paris in 1864 are listed in *Les vues stéréoscopiques* 1992, 33–34); Cousin-Montauban 1932, 337.
9. Legrand may be the man identified as Ligelang by Wang (1862, 122).
10. See also Théodore de Banville's foreword in Fauchery's *Lettres d'un Mineur* (1857).
11. SHAT, G^5-9 "Campagne de Chine." Orders nos. 207 and 215 of 1 July 1860 to 689 of 7 September 1860. Fauchery's presence was confirmed by Colonel Du Pin (1868, 6).
12. Letters dated 13 October and 10 November 1860, published on 28 December 1860 and 16 January 1861.
13. See Dunne (1861, 146) about "looking over Signor Beato's photographs" under the Beijing walls on 23 October 1860.

14. See a forty-four page album in the National Archives in Washington, D.C., thirteen prints in the Peabody Essex Museum collections, and White 1982.
15. For example, Beijing represents thirty-one out of a total of sixty-six views in the Campaign album of Sir Hope Crealock, Elgin's aide-de-camp (now in the collections of the Australian National Gallery, Canberra. See I. Crombie 1987.)
16. Nos. 43 to 48 on the Hering list.
17. The pavilions were not found in the Western enclosure. If they belonged in the Chinese garden (which is doubtful), they would be the only photographs of the garden before the fire. They are nos. 48 and 50 in album C779 H435, Peabody Essex Museum. The *ILN* dated the image of a pavilion (Fig. 5) to 18 October 1860, the day the fire was started.
18. Shelfmark C915.12 P379.9, Peabody Essex Museum, two albums for a total of 125 photographs. They are inscribed on the cover "1861," certainly the starting date of the collection. Several of the images also appear in the collection of the Oriental Museum, Durham, U.K., possibly connected with the Chinese art historian Stephen W. Bushell (private communication from Nick Pearce).
19. On the contribution of photography to the exhibition, and on the actual value of such medals, see McClauley 1994, 87–91.
20. P. Champion, "La Chine et le Japon." See also B. Marbot and R. Viénet 1978, 17–19.
21. At 27 x 33 cm, Champion's plates were larger than average (Champion 1867, 13), which makes identification easier (see p. 135.)
22. For Champion's career with the CNAM, see Archives Nationales, CNAM, *Personnel et matériel, carton* F^{12} 4959. His file was not updated in 1870–71, the time of the Franco-Prussian war and the Siege of Paris.
23. In 1864, *Le Tour du Monde* had already published a number of architectural views of Beijing (see Bourboulon), which is probably why they went for a different approach in this second large article.
24. The only other mention of Morache's photographic work, in the catalog of G.E. Morrison's library, reads "Album 29 large photographs [. . .] each with Ms description in French written by Dr. G.E. Morache" (Morrison 1924). It is unclear whether the entry implies that only the inscription is credited to Morache. "Large" is also interesting in connection with Champion. On the other hand, several other views attributed to Morache are very close, but not identical, to Champion's. There could either have been two photographers working side by side, or a camera moved by a few steps, although this is less likely; considering how difficult and expensive it was to procure plates and chemicals in Beijing, they were not wasted. In any case, there are not enough clues to decide whether they were really made at the same time.
25. See album X12, Peabody Essex Museum.
26. This work was subsequently reprinted under various presentations, and Thomson's collection of negatives was preserved. About 680 plates and fragments are kept by the Wellcome Foundation for the History of Medicine in London: see John Thomson (1991).
27. See also Freeman-Mitford 1900, vi and Devéria 1876:2, 367.

CHAPTER 2

1. The well-publicized Comte de Beauvoir's account (1872), that of a very young man whose trip to China in 1867 allowed him to confirm prejudices rather than to discover a different culture, was an example we would wish isolated, but which was common. For a resident's negative review of the work, see *NCH* 10 August 1872, 106–107.
2. Fifty-five names are listed; but of these, nine were "absent", that is, not residing in Beijing.

3. *The Chronicle and Directory for China, Japan and the Philippines*, first published in Hong Kong by *The China Mail* in 1860, developed in pace with the open, or "treaty" ports. Soon published yearly, and together with its regional version, *The China Directory*, it listed the (mostly, but not exclusively, Western) foreigners and their businesses in China. A similar venture was the *Shanghai Hong List* (Western businesses) in Shanghai. This type of directory was common in East and South Asia, and, despite unavoidable inaccuracies, is very useful to researchers. Unfortunately, most often, only initials were supplied for the first names. In addition, information was not collected but supplied (not everyone can be traced), and only men and the very rare working women were mentioned. To compensate for the latter deficiency, the *Shanghai Ladies Directory* (also known as the *Blue Book*), was created in 1868 when the female population became significant. By the turn of the century, the Directory had become unable to list everyone and was more selective.
4. The society's address was Yuen Ming Yuen street, behind the British consulate. This reminder by the British municipality of Shanghai of the destruction of the Summer Palace was certainly unnecessary from a Chinese point of view; to this day the Rape of the Palace is still brought up in diplomatic discussions.
5. Wilkinson came to Beijing soon after the first photographs of the European Palaces were made. He wrote (1885) an intelligent and witty description of everyday life for a young student-interpreter attached to the British legation, which was very similar to that enjoyed in the Inspectorate General of the Customs by the photographers.
6. Deeply offensive actions included the French Admiral Protêt sneaking into the imperial palace grounds through an open gate and riding up Coal Hill in October 1861 (Rennie 1865, 119), or members of the British legation forcing entrance into the Temple of Heaven grounds in 1868, and playing there a game of cricket (Freeman-Mitford, 1900, 129).
7. See Bredon 1920, Perckhammer 1928, H. Morrison 1985, etc.

CHAPTER 3

1. The techniques summarized here were studied in a number of contemporary or recent works. For easy reference, see Baldwin (1991).
2. "On the requisites necessary for the production of a good photograph," paper read before the Nottingham Photographic Society by L. Bourne, as reported in *The Photographic News* (24 February 1860, 296–8).
3. They were in line with the publication by the British *Photographic News*, of a fascinating account of the wanderings through the interior of Japan in 1858 of a photographer in Japanese disguise. The technical and safety problems faced by this anonymous Norwegian were very similar to those encountered in China at the time. The first article appeared in no. 57 of 7 October 1859, and went on for twenty-one issues.
4. Non-specialized mail-order companies were also active on the market. For example, the 1897 Sears Roebuck catalogue had twelve pages on cameras and photography-related equipment. Advice on the material needed in connection with the type of photography practiced was also available.
5. For illegal copies, see *"L'art et la photographie"* ("Art and Photography") in *La Chronique des Arts et de la Curiosité* (1 February 1863, 107). *Le Tour du Monde* started in 1895 an occasional column, "Advice to travellers, photography and travel," which in 1902 studied the yet-to-be-born color travel photography.
6. In Shanghai, the *NCH* regularly printed items on East Asian photographic activities. They reviewed the series of views made by Beato during the U.S. China Squadron campaign in Korea (1 July 1871), John Thomson's Shanghai slide show on antiquities of Cam-

bodia (18 January 1872), and studied the developments of a diplomatic incident caused by Baron Raimund von Stillfried when photographing the Mikado without authorization (25 January to 29 February 1872).

7. The *NCH* editor's hopes were not strong when he saw a copy, however. On 28 August 1868, he welcomed recent changes to the editorial content and a monthly periodicity.
8. On the limitations of early Chinese photography, see also Long Chin-san [ca. 1978].

CHAPTER 4

1. Such was the case for Lord Macartney when he was sent in embassy to the Qianlong emperor by King George III of England (1793), and the Dutch-American self-styled "ambassador" Van Braam Hougheest, who in 1794 insisted to no avail on seeing the European Palaces of which so much had been heard in Europe since their creation. For the Jesuit descriptions, as well as the embassies in connection with the Yuanmingyuan, see Pirazzoli-t'Serstevens as per bibliography. The American connection of Van Braam, who became American in 1784 but died in Holland, is detailed in Lee (1984, 81–82).
2. In addition, it is clear that access to the ruins was not always possible (see Rennie 1876, 36–37). From about 1886, the Yuanmingyuan became fully out of bounds to visitors, an effective closure brutally concluded by the arrival of the allied troops in 1900 and a second looting of imperial property.
3. This is how it was sketched by the French diplomat Gabriel Devéria in the 1860s ([Devéria] 1876:2, 230).
4. At least the heads were taken to Europe. Five of them were auctioned by Sotheby's in recent years: in New York, 9 October 1989 (monkey and pig), and London, 13 June 1991 (horse, tiger and ox). They apparently came from French collections.

CHAPTER 5

1. For history and use of the European Palaces, see Pirazzoli-t'Serstevens as per bibliography.
2. For structure and organization of the European Palaces, see Durand as per bibliography.
3. The painting illustrates the popularity enjoyed by exotic decoration in mid-eighteenth century Chinese court circles. See for example Uitzinger 1993.
4. This was described by a French court painter who later worked on the European Palaces, the Jesuit Jean-Denis Attiret. His letter was published in France (1749) and England (1765), and attracted considerable attention from the learned world.

CHAPTER 6

1. On the British side, foot soldiers were not allowed in for fear of the type of unrest seen in Delhi during the Sepoy Rebellion (Wolseley 1862, 237–6), but there were no attempts to stop the cavalry.
2. "English newspapers gave of what happened near Beijing, on the occasion of the capture of the Emperor's Summer Palace, fully inaccurate accounts." *Le Siècle*, 20 December 1860.
3. Ironically, the first such paper (by the photographer Antoine Fauchery), was printed in *Le Moniteur Universel*, a pro-government newspaper.

4. One example is the 23 February 1861 presentation in *Le Monde Illustré*, of a series of satirical sketches, "Projects for the rebuilding of the Opera" which included a Chinese pavilion, "Project certainly meant as a memento to the Imperial Summer Palace, the Louvre and Windsor of China . . . "
5. Written from exile in Guernsey, "to Captain Butler," on 25 November 1861.
6. See *The Times*, 11–16 March 1874, on Cousin de Montauban's deposition before the Commission probating Napoleon III's Will and debating the ownership of the collection between the nation and the person of the Emperor (the collection is now displayed in the Musée National de Fontainebleau). For an interpretation of the loot and its treatment, see Hevia (1994).
7. For the legend and its implications, see Millward (1994).
8. In the case of the Yuanyingguan it could be accidental, as the ceramic tiles had previously broken and been repaired (hooks are visible on an enlarged 1873 photograph), and moreover the general balance of the outside walls had been upset by the falling of the roofs. (Alone among the large buildings, the Yuanyingguan followed the Chinese system of non load-bearing walls. The wooden columns, which burnt, were essential to the stability of the structure.)
9. The numbers are not Chinese but Arabic (see Appendix 5, under "characteristics"), suggesting a Western hand, or at least Western prospective buyers. However, the Throne slabs were acquired by the Manchu prince "Tao-pei" in the 1920s (Adam 1936, 42). They are now back on the site.

CHAPTER 7

1. For the organization of the Service in the 1870s, see the Inspector General's Circular No. 25, 1869, on "Rules and regulations for the administration of the Imperial Maritime Customs of China". Despite changes due to development, this remained the basic structure. See "First Series: 1861–1875, IV," *Service Series no 7*, Shanghai, Statistical Department of the Inspectorate General, 1879.
2. See also §7 of Circular No. 25, 1869, and Hart to E.B. Drew, 31 March 1883 (Morse Papers, Harvard).
3. See bibliography.
4. Now respectively in Hildesheim, Germany; Oslo, Norway; and Washington, D.C.
5. See Black (1989). Möllendorf started the Korean customs service.

CHAPTER 8

1. Osman's articles (1989) dealt mostly with Child's life in England; he was the source for the non-Chinese part of this chapter. Marbot and Viénet (1978), authors of an exhibition catalogue on early photographs of China at the Bibliothèque Nationale, listed ninety-two prints by Child, including seven of the European Palaces (the largest number recorded in any single place). Goodrich and Cameron (1978) presented five photographs by Child (spelled "Childe"; in addition, p. 110 was not Child's). Finally, Worswick and Spence included Child in their list of photographers active in China (1978, 150).
2. Because mining coal locally was prohibited at that time, Hart had to import coal for the gas works from England (Hart 1975, 119).
3. For reasons of reliability, only images produced by Child's own studio should be used for reference, as apparent from the origin or the state of the print. While this provision re-

duces the scope of the study, it eliminates late, tainted copies: not all of Child's work will be identified, but what will be is his. The main items which appear reliable are loose prints at the Royal Ontario Museum, and photographs in albums 6618G at the Library of Congress; Uncat. # 1, Peabody Essex Museum; and 79:0054 at George Eastman House.

4. There are several occurences of signatures appearing in light, that is, written in ink. Number 89 is even found with a "dark" signature in the University Museum, University of Pennsylvania, and a "light" one in the George Eastman House. The signature on No. 207 at George Eastman House seems to be by a different hand, although the image, very similar to No. 208, is certainly Child's.
5. The top of the slip is sometimes titled "In and Around Peking, A description of views taken by Thos. Child." This title may have been cut off whenever space was missing on the album page.
6. While the signature is the inscription most likely to be overwritten, a copy of No. 79 at the Library of Congress (6618G, pl. 31) shows a rare dark cursive inscription reading "Scene on the Ha-ta-men Street," covered at the Bibliothèque Nationale (Eo 103) with "No. 79. STREET VIEW. PEKING."
7. Available at the *Far East* offices in Shanghai, copies were 50 cents a piece.
8. There is no trace of an updated list. However, the covers, on which the list is found, were removed upon binding from all four sets of the journal traced for 1878 during this study and *The Far East* had folded by January 1879.
9. While the two views show the same area of the wall, in 1875 Child photographed only one (Western) man, while in 1877 a larger party includes women, and, surprisingly, a babe in arms.
10. For example, the copy of "Wan Shou Shan North," Child No. 3, is found only initialed at the Peabody Essex Museum (EI box 18); the two letters are completed into "T. Child" at the Bibliothèque Nationale (Oe 103).
11. "Yung Lo's (Yongle) tomb at the Ming Tombs, Peking," July 1877; "Sledges used on the Northern Rivers, in Winter," and "The Pekingese Car," December 1877; "Portion of the Great Wall of China," January 1878, and "View of the Dagoba on the Tien-ling-sze (Tianningsi), Celestial Influence Temple, lying west of Peking," November 1878. This last photograph was not credited, as comments were announced but never printed.
12. Interestingly, the engravings were done in the Chinese mode. See for example p. 363 (ed. 1898) the "*Bouddha vivant sur son estrade*," copying the center of Child's No. 184 "Great Lama and Attendants."
13. There were nine photoengravings in the 1898 (second) edition; the 1897 edition presented only four images. All plates were clearly signed "K. Ogawa," probably the engraver. The 1900 and 1902 editions, printed in France, copied only the woodblock engravings, which do not include the European Palaces.

CHAPTER 9

1. [K. Ohlmer] states that he was in Shanghai. However, *The Chronicle and Directory* for 1868 and for 1869 list him as a photographer in Amoy.
2. See King 1924, Arlington 1931, and Spinney Papers.
3. Album Wd 252, Société de Géographie, Bibliothèque Nationale, Paris.
4. Wright (1950) gives precise biographical outlines for a number of Customs officers.
5. *Führer durch die Ernst Ohlmer'sche Sammlung chinesischer Porzellane z. Z. aufgestellt im Roemer-Museum Hildesheim [. . .] mit 10 Tafeln und 3 Zinkographien von E. Ohlmer* (Guide of the Ernst Ohlmer collection of Chinese porcelain currently displayed at the Roemer Museum in Hildesheim, with general comments on Chinese porcelain, its fabrication, its use

and its history [. . .] with 10 plates and 3 zincographs by E. Ohlmer). Architectural views included "*Wan-Schou-Shan Tempel*", pl. II (Zhihuihai in Wanshoushan); "*Einer der Marmorpaläste in Yüan-Ming-Yüan b. Peking, zerstört 1860*", pl. III (Xieqiqu, south); "*Bunte Porzellanbekrönung des Einganges eines Palastes in Yüan-Ming-Yüan*", pl. IV (Yuanyingguan, detail); and "*Seitentheil des Palastes auf Taf. III. mit reicher Porzellanverzierung*", pl. V (east side of Xieqiqu).

6. Oriental Museum, University of Durham, U.K.; Stadtmuseum, Uslar, Germany.
7. The six new images add significantly to photographic sources on the European Palaces. The Uslar prints are kept loose in a portfolio of seven views of the Summer Palace area. The Durham ones, loose and uncredited, belong to another three-view set. With Uslar, this makes a total of ten which apparently belong to the same series, although their mounting is different. The common ground is four of them (two in each set) being printed through the same mask with ornamented top corners. (In opposition to the edge of a print which is always trimmed to some extent, the image created by a printing mask is a signature.)
8. While the name "Ohlmer" on the back is a serious indication, it is disturbing that no copies of these images were ever found together with any of the fifteen Ohlmer views. Were these photographs a second set made by Ohlmer? If so, why did he not keep the negatives with his first set and/or publish any of them? In addition, there is only one area for which there is material for visual comparison between the Uslar-Durham prints and Ohlmer's album—the Xieqiqu. There, the former are slightly later, about Piry's time. Stylistically, the whole is also more evocative of Piry than of what is know of Ohlmer. It could also be a new photographer. Child is not a likely candidate: the images simply do not belong in his academic portfolio, or fit into his list.
9. This date conflicts with the closure for repairs undertaken in the Yuanmingyuan at that time, as indicated by the Qing archives. However, there is no formal proof that, if work was indeed under way by then and the garden officially out of bounds, prohibition of access was really enforced in the European Palaces area, almost opposite from where the Emperor had lived in 1860.
10. The "*Nan-yuan* people" were the Customs Service single men, who lived in mess in the *Nan-yuan* courtyard (as communicated by Dr. Wheeler of the Queen's University Library, Belfast).
11. The limited early coverage of the site does not allow comparison between series beyond the Xieqiqu. It is, however, conceivable that Ohlmer's fifteen views were shot over a period of several years.
12. Piry would be identified through a good photograph dated 1881. There is no reference for Child, but he was then in Beijing as a single man, as his family arrived only in December 1974 (*NCH* 3 December 1874, list of passengers arriving from Nagasaki), and he may very well have been a participant in the outings photographed.
13. Shelfmark "Unserer Katalogrum 45.2:1–52," Museum für Völkerkunde, Hamburg. (The reference was provided by Thomas Theye.)
14. In early China photography, it is more usual to find prints attached on the whole surface or, at least, along the edges.
15. Shelfmark 6618G in Library of Congress; Shelfmark 77.137 in Brooklyn Museum, dated 1871, where photographs are presented after a large set of painted typical scenes from Ningbo (Zhejiang).
16. Kuntsgewerbemuseum and Museum für Volkerkunde, Berlin. However, he may have sold to other museums items which survive: see the set of 1783 engravings of the European Palaces in the National Kunstbibliothek, SMBPK (Berlin). (For the engravings, see p. 130.)
17. See also Wiesner (1981, 9 and 12).
18. The original assemblage of artifacts in the Roemer-Pelizaeus Museum no longer exists.

While the items lent by Ohlmer in 1898 were given to the museum on his death in 1927, the Hanneken family recovered its property after World War II, and the Ohlmer textiles were lost to water damage.

19. Fifty million taels (over 300 million Marks in 1898).
20. The diaries are kept by the architect Ulrich Hausmann in Nottingham, U.K.

CHAPTER 10

1. See H.B. Morse's *Trade and Administration of the Chinese Empire*, in which the chapter on the Postal Service is based on a report by Piry.
2. Unless otherwise specified, the material mentioned in this chapter belongs to the Blackburn collection, Neuilly.
3. The rest of his papers were destroyed, some by fire during the Siege of the Legations in 1900.
4. Sources differ on Piry's position with the Fuzhou Arsenal. But at that time an administrative career in China was not narrowly defined. The director of the arsenal, Prosper Giquel (or Gicquel), came to China as a French naval officer with the French forces in 1857 and learned Chinese. After the campaign of 1860, he was "lent" to the Customs and put in charge of the port of Ningbo (Zhejiang). Soon after, when the port was seized by the Taiping rebels, he fought against them with the "Ever Glorious Army," and finished the campaign in 1864 as head of the army. With Paul d'Aiguebelle, another French Navy officer who had fought against the Taiping rebellion, Giquel then created an arsenal for the purpose of training Chinese to build and sail modern war ships.
5. She wrote her own account of the siege on her return to France (Pons-Laurent [und.]).
6. See for example his 1913 and 1914 private letters to Estrade, of the French *Ministère des Postes* (Letterbooks, Blackburn Collection).
7. For the local conditions, see Arlington (1931, 196–204).
8. The image comes in two formats. Rectangular: Royal Ontario Museum (Toronto), uncat.; Library of Congress (Washington, D.C.), shelfmark 6374H; and Morse (1910–13:1, 602). Oval: Victoria & Albert Museum (London, U.K.), shelfmark 24784; Uslar Stadtmuseum (Germany), uncat.; Ohlmer 1898 (pl. III).
9. On H.B. Morse, see Fairbank 1996.
10. Letters from W.G. Stronach, British consul in Pakhoi, to Sir Thomas Wade in Beijing (London Public Record Office, F.O. 228/631). See also *NCH* (2 September 1879, 232 and 9 September 1879, 250), and Piry to F.A. Schertzer of Canton of 11 December 1879 (Letterbooks).
11. Piry's consumption of photographic plates cannot be precisely estimated. His letterbooks show that a number of orders were not kept, and also that he was supplying "several amateurs of autochromes" in Beijing. In 1909, after a gap in the letterbooks, Lumière was already shipping to Beijing five boxes of four Vérascope (stereographic) plates every fortnight. After an interruption probably due to the Manchuria plague outbreak, Piry reactivated his order in January 1910, raising the quantity to eight boxes. The orders preserved for the period between 3 February 1910 and 26 November 1911 give a total of one hundred fifty-nine boxes of autochromes, all sizes included. How many were for Piry himself? Stereoscopic plates form the bulk of the orders (ninety-one boxes) and almost the whole of his autochrome collection. On the other hand, this was also the time when two major events slowed his activities: the reorganization that followed the separation of the Postal Service from the Customs, and the 1911 revolution. And in fact, there are no orders dated between September 1911 and 13 February 1912 (when he resumed orders with twenty boxes).

CHAPTER 11

1. Most foreign powers were represented in Beijing by ministers, envoys symbolically less important than ambassadors.
2. The diplomat called himself "Alfons von Mumm" in the *Tagebuch*, but the Archives of the German Ministry of Foreign Affairs give him as "Alfons Freiherr Mumm von Schwarzenstein," the correct form after he received his title in 1903. Mumm's career in East Asia has been studied only for Japan (Schwalbe and Seemann 1974, 69–75).
3. A portable camera is seen in the *Tagebuch*, 209, top left. Mumm used glass plates in Italy; see the break visible in a second work, the guidebook *Mein Ligurisches Heim*, 43.
4. The *North China Herald* (11 November 1901, 1123) relates Mumm's visit to Fuzhou. There is also the program (in German and English) of the entertainment specially put together "in honor of the German Guests" at the Fuzhou theater: "Snow White, Dramatized Fairy Tale with songs & dances, in 3 acts." Acting were the German Consul's family and friends (Mrs. Gracey's scrapbook, shelfmark A1979.16a, Peabody Essex Museum).
5. Four examples are pages 45, 152 (lower right) and 263 (top and bottom right), for which albumen prints can be found respectively in the Metropolitan Museum of Art, New York (Album 1991 1073.93), and Royal Ontario Museum, Toronto (loose album leaves), all uncredited. The prints might go back to the 1870s. Whether Mumm ever knew who made them is doubtful.
6. Alfred Dutertre, the chauffeur, still had trouble with his autochrome plates. In Beijing, he received instructions in the art from Théophile Piry, without apparent improvement. See *Commerces d'Asie* 1994, 13.
7. See for example the collection of stereograms offered by the firm Underwood and Underwood in the United States.

CHAPTER 12

1. Only the groups of images larger than five could be considered here. This eliminates Ernst von Perckhammer, author of two views and the most interesting of the "accidental" photographers of this period (see p. 150 n. 2).

   From the start of this study, it was decided not to include the photographs produced by Carroll Brown Malone (pub. 1934) and Maurice Adam (pub. 1936), as they were meant by their authors to support important historical studies of the European Palaces. The only research possible here would have been out of context and could not have done justice to the overall work of the two authors/photographers. Malone and Adam were indeed pioneer researchers on the European Palaces, to whom later authors owe a substantial debt. Incidentally, their photographs do not alter the image of the site given by their predecessors. At best, they would add a new chapter, a chronicle of the massive destructions perpetrated in the 1920s.

   Still, some of their images are unique, such as Malone's view of the theater (Fig. 29.) Born in 1886, Malone was a professor at Qinghua University (Beijing) between 1911 and 1927. In 1928 he presented at the University of Illinois a doctoral thesis on the summer palaces of the Qing emperors which had a large echo and remains a valuable instrument. Maurice Adam (1889–1932), a French resident in Beijing, died before completing his projected work on the European Palaces. Friends compiled a book from the notes and photographs he had collected. They received assistance form Chin Hsün, a librarian at the National Library of Beijing whose family had been architects of the Yuanmingyuan, and who had also done his own research on the site.

   In contrast with the two previous authors, the European Palaces were only a portion of Osvald Sirén's important work on the monuments of Beijing and the Chinese gardens, which justified retaining them. As to Piry's views for 1911–13, they were studied in chapter 10 above. But the six images by Sidney D. Gamble, traced in 1997, are only listed in Appendix 5, as they did not contribute or add significantly to an already completed study.

2. Unless otherwise indicated, the source used for Anner is the Rockefeller Archive Center, North Tarrytown, N.Y. ("C. W. Anner Papers," and "Appropriations 1919–1931").
3. For biographical details, see Anner's "Curriculum Vitae" dated September 10, 1931. For the Rockefeller Foundation's activities in China, see Bullock (1980), and Ferguson (1970).
4. Personal communication from Mrs. Frances Anner in Alexandria (Virginia), in October 1991.
5. Source: Mrs. Anner.
6. Anner, Black, Sirén, Adam (1936), Malone (1934) and the writer George Kates (1988, 197–200) all collected, used or mentioned these engravings. Without going back to the set sent by the Jesuits c. 1785 (see Pirazzoli-t'Serstevens 1989:4, 5), which Delatour, the recipient, studied in *Essais sur l'architecture des Chinois* (Paris 1803), the first (incomplete) set recorded in France after 1860 was purchased in 1890 by the Ecole des Beaux-Arts de Paris (see Thiriez and Durand 1993, 106 and n. 26), while the Victoria & Albert Museum (London) acquired nineteen prints in or before 1883.
7. Plates 12, 32 and 33 in Schulz (1966), the published version of a thesis (the original manuscript was returned to the author by Würzburg University). The handwritten manuscript was loaned to Schulz by Prof. George Loehr. Loehr's library was subsequently dispersed after his death.
8. Plate 7, top, Yuanyingguan. The lower image, of the Haiyantang, probably belongs to the same series.
9. See pp. 139–142, under "characteristics." It should be noted that, although numbers on negatives are an important clue, their absence is not significant. By that time already, prints showed only what was written on the image proper, to the exclusion of the margins on the negatives. Film was not yet perforated; depending on the camera, the negative would, or would not, show a margin large enough for notes. For instance, Carl W. Bishop's negatives at the Freer Gallery are all numbered, but the number is visible on the print only when the margin is reduced (see Fig. 54).
10. Images from this series are currently used in Chinese publications to show the Yuanmingyuan area, unfortunately so far without credit. Furthermore, Fu Gongye (1989) removed the numbers, thus preventing identification of any other prints from the series he may have published in addition to those, already known, of the European Palaces.
11. The photographs are credited in bulk to his collection and to "Herbert Mueller [in China in 1912–1914], Hermann Schoede, Teg.-Baumeister Schubert and Baurat E. Boerschmann," in an acknowledgement dated May 1919. Even supposing the list comprehensive, images need to be checked one by one, an almost impossible feat after WWII's destructions in Germany.
12. The plates face pages 51, 81, 139 (top), 187, 246, 267 and 335 (top). None shows the European Palaces. Dunn was credited with all the plates in bulk, a common but often misleading practice.
13. In 1916, the University Museum, University of Pennsylvania, spent $160.000 from private contributions in field trip expenses.
14. Unless otherwise specified, the details relating to Bishop's 1915–17 expedition were found in the Bishop Papers in the Archives of the University Museum, University of Pennsylvania, Philadelphia.
15. Nos. C156 to C229: fourteen objects from Japan and fifty-nine from China (most of them Han and pre-Tang *mingqi*–funerary items).

16. "Among other things, I have been diligent in securing as fine a collection of photographs of all kinds as possible . . . " (Bishop to Gordon, 14 August 1917).
17. Nos. 22–192–1 to 14, Japanese earthenware or stone Neolithic objects.
18. Bishop's collecting activities for U.S. museums have been studied by Cohen (1992).
19. The biographical notes rely on Sirén's letter of 19 November 1955 to A.G. Wenley, Director of the Freer Gallery of Art, which discussed the award in 1956 of the Charles Freer Lang Medal to Sirén (Freer Gallery of Art Central Files, Archives, as communicated by Colleen Hennessey.)
20. This work will leave to other researchers the sizeable task of analyzing Sirén's contribution to his chosen field. Such a study is under way in Canada. Accordingly, only the photographs of the European Palaces are considered here.
21. See Appendix 5 under "Characteristics."

CONCLUSION

1. A letter from Sirén to Bishop dated 24 February 1930, when they were both in Beijing, referred to an "old acquaintance" between them (Bishop Papers, AFGA).
2. The following conclusions take into account Gamble and Perckhammer, but they do not apply to Hedda Morrison, who was not part of either period or study. It can be noted, in fact, that Morrison's case contradicts many of the following statements. Still, she was a German, learned Chinese, and her photographs of the European Palaces were personal records (personal communication of 15 April 1990).
3. This is made clear by Adam's and Malone's selection of documents to illustrate their study of the European Palaces in the 1920s (see chap. 12, n. 1): the only early photographs they used were Child's as published by Favier in 1897–8. Neither considered any other source, although even contemporaries such as Anner, Black and Bishop would have provided views very relevant to their demonstration.

APPENDIX 3

1. A single sketch of a detail of the Haiyantang, the largest European palace, has been attributed without safe basis to Giuseppe Castiglione, the Jesuit painter who was in charge of the project. Reproduced in Favier's *Peking*.
2. Adam 1936. See also the special issue on the Yuanmingyuan of the *Bulletin of the National Library of Peiping* nos. 3–4 (May-August 1933): 119–176.
3. On the reliability of the engravings as sources, see Thiriez and Durand, 1993.

BIBLIOGRAPHY

Photographic Repositories Consulted

Agence Roger-Viollet, Paris, France

Arnold Arboretum, Boston, Mass., U.S.A.

Boston Athæneum, Boston, Mass., U.S.A.

Charles Blackburn, Neuilly, France

Bibliothèque nationale de France, Departement des Estampes, Paris, France

Brooklyn Museum of Art

Earl of Elgin Archives, Dumfermline, Fife, Scotland

Freer Gallery of Art-Arthur M. Sackler Gallery, Washington, D.C., U.S.A.

Sidney D. Gamble Archives, The Sidney D. Gamble Foundation for China Studies, New York, N.Y., U.S.A.

International Museum of Photography at George Eastman House, Rochester, N.Y., U.S.A.

G. Paul Getty Museum, Malibu, CA, U.S.A.

Harvard-Yenching Library, Cambridge, Mass., U.S.A.

Library of Congress, Washington, D.C., U.S.A.

Metropolitan Museum of Art, Prints and Drawings Department, New York, U.S.A.

Musée Albert Kahn, Boulogne-Billancourt, France

Musée de l'Homme, Paris, France

Musée d'Orsay, Paris, France

Musée national des Arts asiatiques–Guimet, Paris, France

Museum für Volkerkunde, Hamburg, Germany

National Archives, Washington, D.C., U.S.A.

National Photographic Collection, Victoria & Albert Museum, London, U.K.

National Museum of Denmark, Department of Ethnology, Copenhagen, Denmark

National Army Museum, London, U.K.

Durham University Oriental Museum, Durham, U.K.

Östasiatiska Museet, Stockholm, Sweden

Peabody Essex Museum, Salem, Mass., U.S.A.

Queen's University Library, Belfast, U.K.

Royal Ontario Museum, Far Eastern Department, Toronto, Canada

School of Oriental and African Studies, University of London, London, U.K.

Stadtmuseum, Uslar, Germany

Société de Géographie at Bibliothèque nationale de France, Paris, France

University Museum Archives, University of Pennsylvania Archives, Philadelphia, PA, U.S.A.

Victoria & Albert Museum, Photographic Collection, London, U.K.

Wellcome Institute for the History of Medicine, London, U.K.

Archival Repositories Consulted

Archives Nationales, Paris, France

"Conservatoire des Arts et métiers, personnel et matériel, 1850–1869," cartons F^{12} 5770–5772:"Conseil de perfectionnement, personnel, matériel, inventions An IV-1879," cartons F^{12} 4859–4866

Charles Blackburn, Neuilly, France

Théophile Piry's archives and photographs

Earl of Elgin Papers, Dumfermline, Fife, U.K.

"Archives of the Eight Earl of Elgin" for 1858–1864

"Archives of Sir Frederick Bruce" for 1858–1864

Freer Gallery of Art-Arthur M. Sackler Gallery ("FGA"), Washington, D.C., U.S.A.

"Carl W. Bishop Papers," archives and photographs
"Benjamin March Papers," photographs

Harvard-Yenching Library, Harvard, Cambridge, Mass., U.S.A.

"J.K. Fairbank Papers"

Houghton Library, Harvard, Cambridge, Mass., U.S.A.

"Hosea B. Morse Papers," Ms Chinese 3–5

Ministère des Affaires Etrangères, Paris, France

List of correspondence for consular and commercial affairs, and for posts and telegraphs

Peabody Essex Museum ("PEM"), Salem, Mass, U.S.A.

"Annie Ward Spinney Papers"

Acquisition Records

Public Records Office, London, U.K.

Foreign Official Reports, FO 228/631, Pakhoi

Queen's University Library, Belfast, U.K.

"Sir Robert Hart's Papers," letters and photographs

"Stanley F. Wright Papers"

Rockefeller Archive Center, North Tarrytown, N.Y., U.S.A.

"Conrad W. Anner Papers"

"Appropriations 1920–1941"

Royal Engineers Regiment, Chatham, Kent, U.K.

Papers on the 1860 China Campaign; photographs

School of Oriental and African Studies, London, U.K.

Papers relating to the Chinese Maritime Customs, 1860–1943

"Papers relating to the Bowra family and its service with the Chinese Maritime Customs, 1840–1966", boxes 17–20

Archives of the Council for World Mission, photographs

Service Historique de l'Armée de Terre (SHAT), Vincennes, France

G[5], Expédition de Chine, 1858–1864

Personal files for Charles Dupin (8301), Maurice Irisson (27330/N), and Georges Morache (80415/N)

Service Historique de la Marine, Vincennes, France

"Arsenal de Fou-tchéou (Fuzhou), 1866–1877, 1890," carton BB4 1555

Personal files for Prosper Giquel (CC 7 1020) and Louis Dunoyer de Segonzac (CC 7 2728)

University Museum Archives ("UMA"), University of Pennsylvanie, Philadelphia, PA, U.S.A.

Bishop, C.W., Journal (20.3.1917–16.1.1918) and Correspondance (1914–1927), East Asia

Nineteenth Century Newspapers and Journals

The British Journal of Photography (BJP), London (consulted 1858–1862)

Bulletin de la Société française de photographie (BSFP), Paris (1855–80)

China Directory, Hong Kong (1860–1920)

China Magazine, Hong Kong (1868–69)

La Chine Nouvelle, Paris (1899–1901)

Chronicle and Directory for China, Japan and the Philippines (with which is incorporated the "China Directory"), Hong Kong (1860–1930)

Customs' Gazette, Shanghai (1869–1920)

The Far East, Yokohama (1870–1875), Shanghai (1876–1878)

The Graphic, London (1880–1898)

Illustrated London News (ILN), London (1855–1925)

L'Illustration, Paris (1855–1920)

Jahrbuch für Photografie und Reproduktionstechnik (1887–1902)

Le Monde Illustré, Paris (1858–1870)

Le Moniteur universel, Paris (1859–61)

North China Daily News (NCDN), Shanghai (1870–74)

North China Herald (NCH), Shanghai (1862–1880)

Photographic News (PN) (1858–1862)

Service Lists of the Maritime Customs, Shanghai (1869 *et seq.*)

Le Siècle (1860–1862)

Le Temps (17/3/1861 and following issues)

The Times (1859–1861, 1874)

Le Tour du monde (TDM), Paris (1860–1915)

Year-Book of Photography and Photographic News Almanac, London (1891)

Books and Articles

Adam, Maurice. *Yuen Ming Yuen: l'œuvre architecturale des anciens jésuites au XVIIIe siècle.* Peip'ing: Imprimerie des Lazaristes, 1936.

Arlington, L.C. *Through the Dragon's Eyes.* New York: Richard R. Smith, 1931.

Arlington, L.C. and Lewisohn, W. *In search of Old Peking.* Peking: Vetch, 1935.

Attiret, Jean-Denis. "A particular account of the Emperor of China's gardens near Pekin, in a letter from F. Attiret, a French Missionary, now employed by that Emperor to paint the Apartments in those Gardens, to his Friend at Paris." Tr. from the French by Sir Harry Beaumont *alias* Joseph Spence. In *Fugitive Pieces on Various Authors.* Vol. 1. London: J. Dodsley, 1765.

Baldwin, Gordon. *Looking at Photographs; A Guide to Technical Terms.* Malibu: The J. Paul Getty Museum, 1991.

Barmé, Geremie R. "The Garden of Perfect Brightness, A Life in Ruins." *East Asian History,* 11 (1996): 111–158.

Beausoleil, Jeanne, et al. *Les Frères Lumière et les premières photographies en couleurs.* Paris: André Barret, 1989.

Beauvoir, Comte Ludovic de. *Pékin, Yeddo et San Francisco, Voyage autour du Monde.* Paris: Plon, 1872.

Beers, Burton F. *China in Old Photographs: 1860–1910.* New York: Scribner, 1978.

Bind A. *Dansk Biografisk Leksikon.* Copenhagen, 1979.

Black, Kay E. "The Korean Ethnografical Collection at the Peabody Museum of Salem." *Korean Culture,* Winter 1989: 12–33.

Bonnetain, Paul. *L'Extrême-Orient.* Paris: Quantin, 1887, reed 1892 (abbreviated).

Bourboulon, C. de. "Relation de voyage de Shanghai à Moscou, par Pékin, la Mongolie et la Russie asiatique, rédigée d'après les notes de voyage de M. de Bourboulon, Ministre de France en Chine, et de Mme de Bourboulon par M. A. Poussielgue." *Tour du Monde,* 1864–1865.

Bourne, L. (or S.). "On the requisites for the production of a good photograph." *Photographic News,* 4:77 (24 February 1860): 296–8.

Brandt, Max von. *Dreiunddreissig Jahre in Ost-Asien.* 3 vol. Leipzig: Georg Wigand, 1901.

Breckenridge, Carol A. "The Aesthetics and politics of colonial collecting: India at World Fairs." In *Comparative Studies in Society and History,* 31 (1989): 195–216.

Bredon, Juliet. *Peking: A Historical and Intimate Description of its Chief Places of Interest.* Shanghai: Kelly & Walsh, 1920.

Brooks, James. *A Seven Months's Run Up and Down and Around the World.* New York: Appleton, 1872.

Bullock, Mary B. *An American Transplant, the Rockefeller Foundation and Peking Union Medical College.* Berkeley: University of California Press, 1980.

Campbell, R. R. *James Duncan Campbell, A Memoir by his Son.* Harvard East Asian Monographs. Cambridge, Mass: Harvard University Press, 1970.

Capa, C. *Behind the Great Wall of China, Photographs from 1870 to the Present.* Greenwich, CT: Weston J. Naef, 1972.

Champion, Paul. "Clichés destinés aux grossissements." *Bulletin de la Société française de photographie,* 1860: 208.

Champion, Paul. "Remarques sur les difficultés que présente la Photographie dans les contrées telles que la Chine et le Japon." *Bulletin de la Société française de photographie*, 1867: 13–18.

Champion, Paul. "La Chine et le Japon." *Etudes sur l'Exposition de 1867. Annales et archives de l'industrie au XIXème siècle . . .* Paris: Eugène Lacroix, 1869.

Champion, Paul. "Nouvel inflammateur pour torpilles automatiques." *Moniteur scientifique*, 1877.

Child, Thomas. "Peking." *Journal of the Society of Arts*, London, no. 43 (1 February 1895): 201–221.

Child, Thomas. "The oldest observatory in the world." *Pearson's Magazine*, 5:27 (1898).

Chirol, Valentine. *The Far Eastern Question*. London: Macmillan, 1896.

Choutzé, T. see Devéria, Gabriel.

Clunas, Craig. *Chinese Export Watercolours*. London: Victoria & Albert Museum, 1984.

Coe, Brian, and Haworth-Booth, Mark. *A Guide to Early Photographic Processes*. London: Victoria & Albert Museum, 1983.

Coe, Brian. *Cameras: From Daguerreotypes to Instant Pictures*. Gothenburg (Sweden): Nordbok, 1978.

Cohen, Warren I. *East Asian Art and American Culture: A Study in International Relations*. New York: Columbia University Press, 1992.

Combaz, Gisbert. "Les palais impériaux de la Chine." *Annales de la Société archéologique de Bruxelles*, 21, nos. 3–4 (1908): 425–583.

Commerces d'Asie. *Autochromes & Noir et blanc 1908–1927*. Boulogne-Billancourt: Musée Albert Kahn, 1994.

Cousin-Montauban, Charles, Comte de Palikao. *L'Expédition de Chine de 1860. Souvenirs du Général Cousin de Montauban, Comte de Palikao*. Paris: Plon, 1932 .

Crammer-Byng, J.L. "The Old British Legation at Peking." *Journal of the Royal Asiatic Society*, Hong Kong Branch, 3 (1963): 60–87.

Crombie, Isobel. "China, 1860: A Photographic Album by Felice Beato." *History of Photography*, 2: 1 (1987): 25–37.

Crouch, Archie R., et al. *Christianity in China: A Scholar's Guide to Resources in Libraries & Archives of the United States*. Armonk, New York & London: M.E. Sharpe, 1989.

Dennys, N.B. *Notes for Tourists in the North of China*. Hong Kong: Shortrede, 1866.

Devéria, Gabriel [*alias* Choutzé, T.] "Pékin et le nord de la Chine." *Tour du Monde*, 1876.

Devéria, Gabriel [*alias* Choutzé, T.], and Thomson, John. *La Cina*. Milano: Treves, 1895.

Droguet, Vincent, "Les Palais Européens de l'empereur Qianlong et leurs sources italiennes." *Histoire de l'Art*, May 1994: 15–28.

Dumoulin, Eugène. *Manuel élémentaire de photographie au collodion humide à l'usage des commencants*. Paris: Gauthier-Villars, 1874.

Dumoulin, Eugène. *La photographie sans laboratoire, procédé au gélatino-bromure. tirage des épreuves positives, temps de pose, épreuves instantanées*. Paris, Gauthier-Villars, 1886.

Dunne, Hart. *From Calcutta to Peking, Being Notes Taken from the Journal of an Officer Between Those Places*. London: Sampson Low, 1861.

Du Pin, Colonel. *Le Japon*. Paris: A. Bertrand, 1868.

Du Pin, Colonel, see also Varin, Paul.

Durand, Antoine. *Restitution des Palais européens du Yuanmingyuan*. Mémoire de Diplôme, Ecole d'Architecture Paris Villemin, 1988, unpub.

Durand, Antoine. "Restitution des Palais Européens du Yuanmingyuan." *Arts Asiatiques*, 43 (1988): 122–133.

Edwards, G. *International Guide to Nineteenth Century Photography*. Boston: G.K. Hall, 1988.

Enders, Elizabeth C. *Swinging Lanterns*. New York: Appleton & Co., 1923.

Fabre, Charles. *Traité encyclopédique de photographie*. 4 vol. & suppl. Paris: Gauthier-Villars, 1889.

Fairbank, John K. *Trade and Diplomacy on the China Coast: The Opening of the Treaty Ports, 1842–1854*. 2 vol. Cambridge, Mass: 1953.

Fairbank, John K. *H.B. Morse, Customs Commissioner and Historian of China*. Lexington: University Press of Kentucky, 1996.

Falconer, John. "John Ashton Papillon: An Amateur Photographer in China 1858–60." *The Photographic Collector*, 3, no. 3 (1982): 346–362.

Fauchery, Antoine. *Lettres d'un mineur en Australie*. Paris: Poulet-Malassis-De Broisse, 1857.

Fauchery, Antoine. "Lettres de Chine." *Moniteur Universel*, 12 October 1860 to 3 February 1861.

Favier, Alphonse. *Péking, histoire et description*. Péking: Impr. Lazaristes, 1897. reed. 1898; Lille: Société de Saint Augustin, 1900; Lille: Desclée de Brouwer, 1902.

Favier, Alphonse. *Lettres d'Alphonse Favier (Prêtre de la Mission de St Lazare) à sa famille–depuis son départ pour la Chine*. v.1. [uns., und.]

Ferguson, Mary E. *China Medical Board and Peking Union Medical College*. New York: China Medical Board of New York, 1970.

Fischer, Emil. *Guide to Peking and its Environs, by Fei-shi*. Tientsin: Tientsin Press, 1909, repr. 1924.

Freeman-Mitford, A.B. *The Attaché at Peking*. London: Macmillan, 1900.

Fu Gongye, ed. *Old Beijing in Panorama*. Beijing, Zhenmin Zhonguo Chubanshi, 1992.

Genest, Gilles. "Les Palais européens du Yuanmingyuan : essai sur la végétation des jardins." *Arts Asiatiques*, 49 (1994): 82–90.

Gill, Arthur T. *Obits: An Alphabetical Listing of the Obituaries Published in the BJA and the Photographic Journal up to 1979*, Ms.

Gimon, Gilbert. "Jules Itier, Daguerreotypist." *History of Photography*, 5, no. 5 (July 1981) 225–239.

Giquel, Prosper. *L'arsenal de Fou-tchéou et ses résultats*. Shanghai: A.M. de Carvalho, 1874.

Goodrich, L. C. "Carl Whiting Bishop, 1881–1942." [und., unp.].

Goodrich, L. Carrington, and Cameron, Nigel. *The Face of China as Seen by Photographers & Travellers, 1860–1912*. Millerton, NY: Aperture, 1978.

Guide Nagel. *Chine*. 4th ed. Geneva, 1980.

Hall, B. Foster. *The Chinese Maritime Customs: An International Service, 1854–1950*, Maritime Monographs and Reports, No. 26, National Maritime Museum, Greenwich, 1977.

Hanneken, Constantin von. "Episoden aus dem chinesisch-japanischen Kriege." *Deutsche Rundschau* 86–87 (1896).

Hart, Robert. *Robert Hart and China's Early Modernization: His Journals, 1863–1866*. Smith R.J., Fairbank J.K., Bruner K.E., ed., Harvard East Asian Monographs, no. 155. Cambridge, Mass: Harvard University Press, 1991.

Hart, Robert. *Entering China's Service; Robert Hart's Journals*. Bruner K.E., Fairbank J.K., Smith R.J., ed., Harvard East Asian Monographs, no. 125. Cambridge, Mass: Harvard University Press, 1986.

Hart, Robert. *The I.G. in Peking: Letters of Robert Hart, Chinese Maritime Customs, 1868–1907*. 2 vol. Fairbank, John K. et al., ed. Cambridge, Mass: The Bellknap Press, 1975.

Hering, H. *Collection of Photographic Views and Panoramas Taken by Signor F. Beato During the Indian Mutiny . . . and the Late War in China . . .* London, c. 1861.

Hérisson, Comte d'. *Journal d'un interprète en Chine*. 3rd ed. Paris: P. Ollendorf, 1886.

Hevia, James L. "Loot's Fate, The Economy of Plunder and the Moral Life of Objects 'From the Summer Palace of the Emperor of China'." *History of Anthropology*, 6, no. 4 (1994): 319–345.

Hornby, Joan. "De 'Europæiske Paldser': Peking Kinas svas på 1700-tallets euroæiske Kineserier." *Nationalmuseets Arbejdsmark*, Copenhagen, 1986: 5–25.

Huang T., Huang Z. *Yuanmingyuan*. Hongkong: Salian Shudian, 1985.

Hübner, Baron J.A. von. *A Ramble Round the World, 1871*. New York: Macmillan, 1875.

Hugo, Victor. "Lettre au capitaine Butler." Dated 25 November 1861, repr. in *Courrier de l'Unesco*, November 1985: 14.

Johnson, William S., ed. *Nineteenth Century Photography: An Annotated Bibliography, 1839–1879*. Boston: G.K. Hall, 1990.

Kates, George N. *The Years that Were Fat*. 1952, repr. Hong Kong: Oxford University Press, 1988.

King, Paul H. *In the Chinese Customs Service: a Personal Record of Forty-Seven Years*. London: T. Fisher Unwin, 1924.

Knollys, Henry. *Incidents in the China War of 1860, Compiled from the Private Journals of Sir Hope Grant*. Edinburgh & London: W. Blackwood & Sons, 1875.

"L'art et la photographie." *Chronique des arts et de la curiosité*, 1 (1 February 1863): 107.

Laur, Francis. *Siège de Pékin, récits authentiques des assiégés . . .* Paris: Société des publications scientifiques et industrielles, 1904–1905.

Lécuyer, Raymond. *Histoire Générale de la Photographie*. Paris: Baschet, 1945.

Lee, Jean G. *Philadelphians and the China Trade, 1784–1841*. Philadelphia: Philadelphia Museum of Art, 1984.

Leibo, Steven A. *Transferring Technology to China: Prosper Giquel and the Self-Strengthening Movement*. Berkeley: University of California, Center for Chinese Studies, 1985.

Loch, Henry Brougham. *Personal Narrative of Occurences During Lord Elgin's Second Embassy to China, 1860*. London: John Murray, 1869.

Londe, Albert. *La photographie instantanée, théorie et pratique*. Paris: Gauthier-Villars, 1886.

Long, Chin-san as told to Betty Yung. "China and the newfangled invention." *Echo Magazine*, 6, no. 8, [ca. 1978], Taipei.

Lowry, John. "Felice Beato's Mail Order Business." *Country Life*, 13 March 1975: 659–660.

Malone, Carroll Brown. "History of the Peking Summer Palaces under the Ch'ing Dynasty." *Illinois Studies of the Social Sciences*, 19, no. 1–2, University of Illinois, 1934 (repr. 1976).

Marbot, Bernard, and Viénet, René. *La Chine entre le collodion humide et le gélatinobromure.* Paris: Bibliothèque Nationale, 1978.

Marder, William, and Estelle. *Anthony, the Man, the Company, the Cameras.* Amesbury: Pine Ridge Publishing Co., 1982.

Mayers W.F., Dennys N.B., and King C. *The Treaty Ports of China and Japan. A Complete Guide to the Open Ports; with Peking, Yedo, Hongkong and Macao. A Guide Book and Vade Mecum.* London: Trübner & Hong Kong: Shortrede, 1867.

McCauley, Elizabeth A. *Industrial Madness: Commercial Photography in Paris, 1848–1871.* Newhaven and London: Yale University Press, 1994.

"Mélanges." *T'oung Pao,* 1911: 573–75.

M'Ghee, R.J.L. *How We Got to Peking: A Narrative of the Campaign of 1860.* London: R. Bentley, 1862.

Michaud, Stéphane et al. *Usages de l'image au XIXème siècle.* Paris: Créaphis, 1992.

Millward, James A. "A Uyghur Muslim in Qianlong's Court: The Meanings of the Fragrant Concubine. " *Journal of Asian Studies,* 53, no. 2 (May 1994): 427–458.

Moges, Marquis de. *Souvenirs d'un voyage en Chine et au Japon en 1857 et 1858.* Paris: Hachette, 1860.

Morache, Georges. *Pékin et ses habitants, études d'hygiène.* Paris: Baillière et fils, 1869, repr. from *Annales d'hygiène publique et de médecine légale,* 1868: 38.

Morrison, Alastair. "Hedda Morrison in Peking: a personal recollection." *East Asian History* no. 4 (December 1992): 105–118.

Morrison, George E. *Catalogue of the Asiatic Library of Dr. G.E. Morrison (now a part of the Oriental Library, Tokyo, Japan).* 2 vol. Tokyo: Oriental Library, 1924.

Morrison, G.E. *The Correspondence of G.E. Morrison.* 2 vol. Lo-Hui-min, ed. Cambridge, Mass: Cambridge University Press, 1976–78.

Morrison, Hedda. *A Photographer in Old Peking.* Hong Kong: Oxford University Press, 1985.

Morrison, Hedda. *Travels of a Photographer in China.* Hong Kong: Oxford University Press, 1987.

Morse, Hosea Ballou. *The Trade and Administration of the Chinese Empire.* London: Longmans, Green, 1908.

Morse, Hosea Ballou. *The International Relations of the Chinese Empire.* 3 vol. Shanghai: Kelly & Walsh, 1910–1913.

Mumm, Alfons Freiherr von. *Ein Tagebuch in Bildern.* Berlin, [ca. 1902].

Mumm, Alfons Freiherr von. *Mein ligurisches Heim.* Berlin: Büxenstein, [ca. 1915].

Musso, Giuseppe D. *La Cina ed i Cinesi, loro leggi e costumi.* 2 vol. Milano: U. Hoepli, 1926.

Negretti & Zambra. *Descriptive Catalogue of Stereoscopic Views of China, from Negatives Taken by the Wet Collodion Process, and Printed and Published by Negretti & Zambra, Photographers to the Crystal Palace, 107, Holborn Hill; 1 Hatton Garden; and 59, Cornhill.*

Ohlmer, Ernst. *Tsingtau, sein Handel und sein Zoll-System.* Tsingtau, 1913.

Ohlmer, Ernst. *Stand und Aufgaben der deutschen Industrie in Ostasien. Ein Weck- und Mahnruf an dieselbe.* Hildesheim, 1905, foreword M. von Brandt.

[Ohlmer, Ernst]. *Führer durch die Ernst Ohlmer'sche Sammlung chinesischer Porzellane z. Z. aufgestellt im Roemer-Museum Hildesheim. mit 10 Tafeln und 3 Zinkographien von E. Ohlmer.* Hildesheim: Gerstenberg, 1898.

Ohlmer, Karl. *Das Geschlecht Ohlmer aus Norsdtemmen, Geschichte un Geschlechterreihen 1593–1932.* [und.]

Osman, Colin. "In Search of Thomas Child." *British Journal of Photography,* 3 to 24 August 1989.

Pauthier, Guy. "Des curiosités chinoises exposées aux Tuileries." *Gazette des Beaux-Arts,* 15 March 1861: 363–369.

Perckhammer, Heinz von. *Eine Nachteit in China.* Berlin: Eingenbrodler Verlag, [1928].

Perckhammer, Heinz von. *Peking. Das Gesicht einer Stadt.* Berlin: Albertus Verlag, 1928.

Perckhammer, Heinz von. *Von China und Chinesen.* Zürich: Orell Füssli-Verlag, 1930.

Perzynski, Friedrich von. *Von Chinas Göttern: Reisen in China.* München: Kurt Wolff Verlag, 1920.

Pirazzoli-t'Serstevens, Michèle, ed. *Le Yuanmingyuan, jeux d'eau et palais européens du XVIIIème siècle à la cour de Chine.* With A. Chayet, A. Durand, P. Jonathan, M-R Paupe, M. Pradayrol, D. Rabreau. Paris: Editions Recherche sur les Civilisations, A.D.P.F., 1987 (text in French and Chinese, English summary).

Pirazzoli-t'Serstevens, Michèle. "The Emperor Qianlong's European Palaces." *Orientations,* November 1988: 61–71.

Pirazzoli-t'Serstevens, Michèle. "A Pluridisciplinary Research on Castiglione and the Emperor Ch'ien-lung's European Palaces." *National Palace Museum Bulletin* (1989) 24: 4 (1–12), 5 (1–16).

Piry, A. Théophile. *Le Saint Edit, étude de littérature chinoise.* Shanghai: Bureau des statistiques, I.G. des Douanes, 1879.

Piry, A. Théophile. *Erh-Tou-Mei ou les pruniers merveilleux, roman chinois traduit et accompagné de notes philologiques.* 2 vol. Paris: E. Dentu, 1880.

Piry, A. Théophile. *Manuel de langue mandarine ou recueil idéologique en chinois, français et anglais des termes, locutions et idiomes de la langue mandarine du nord.* Shanghai: Presse du bureau de la statistique, 1895.

Piry, A. Théophile. "Le peuple chinois et la réforme." *Revue des Deux Mondes,* 1901:3, 656–676.

Pons-Laurent, Mme S. *Siège de Pékin, 19 juin-14 août 1900.* Cannes: Louis Vidal, und.

Reilly, Dianne, and Carew, Jennifer. *Sun Pictures of Victoria: The Fauchery-Daintree Collection, 1858.* Victoria, Australia: Curry O'Neill Ross, 1983.

Reilly, Dianne. *The Life and Times of Antoine Fauchery.* Melbourne, MA Thesis, Monash University, 1984, unpub.

Rennie, David F. *The British Arms in China and Japan: Peking 1860; Kagosima 1862.* London, 1862.

Rennie, David F. *Peking and the Pekingese during the first year of the British Embassy at Peking.* London: J. Murray, 1865.

Rennie, W.G. *Guide for Tourists to Peking and its Environs.* Hongkong: China Mail, 1876, reprint Yientsin press, 1897.

Richard, Pierre Marc. *Société Française de Photographie, membres-correspondants-amateurs-exposants. Index 1854–1876.* Paris: Editions du Palmier en Zinc, 1990.

Roberts, Clare, ed. *In her View: The Photographs of Hedda Morrison in China and Sarawak, 1933–1967.* Haymarket, Australia: Powerhouse Publishing, 1993.

Salu, Luc, and Roosen, Laurent. *History of Photography, A Bibliography of Books*. London and New York: Mansell, 1989.

Schulz, Alexander. *Hsi Yang Lou: Untersuchungen zu den "Europaische Bauten" des Kaiser Ch'ien-lung*. Würzburg: Würzburg Universität, 1966.

Schwalbe, Hans, and Seemann, Heinrich. *Deutsche Botschafter in Japan, 1860–1973*. Tokyo: Deutsche Gesellshaft für Natur- und Völkerkunde Ostasiens, 1974.

Sennett, Robert S. *The Nineteenth-Century Photographic Press: A Study Guide*. New York and London: Garland Publishing, 1987.

Singer, Noel F. *Burmah. A Photographic Journey, 1855–1925*. Stirling: Kiscadale, 1993.

Sirén, Osvald. "A Chinese Emperor Plays Photographer's Assistant." *The New York Times Magazine*, 22 April 1923.

Sirén, Osvald. *Les Palais impériaux de Pékin*. 3 vol. Paris and Bruxelles: Van Oest, 1926 (tr. *The Imperial Palaces of Peking*. Brussels: Van Oest, 1926).

Sirén, Osvald. *Trädgårdar i Kina*. Stockholm, 1948 (tr. *Gardens of China*. New York: Ronald Press, 1949).

Sirén, Osvald. *Bibliographia Osvaldi Sirén*. Stockholm: Nationalmuseui skrifter 6, Natur och Kultur, 1960.

Smith, Albert. *To China and Back*. London: Chapman & Hall, [ca. 1859].

"Some Chinese Pictures." *Blackwood Magazine*, 8 (1869): 271.

Swinhoe, Robert. *Narrative of the North China Campaign of 1860*. London: Smith, Elder, 1861.

Teng gu. *Yuanmingyuan oushi gongdian canji*. Shanghai: Shangwu yinshuguan, 1933.

Thiriez, Régine. "Old Photography and the Yuanmingyuan." In *Art History Through the Camera's Lens*. New York: Gordon and Breach Science Publishers, 1995: 263–280 (repr. from *Visual Resources*, 6 (1990)).

Thiriez, Régine. *Les photographes occidentaux des Palais européens du Yuanmingyuan, 1860–1925*. Ph.D. dissertation, Ecole Pratique des Hautes Etudes, Section Etudes Historiques et Philogiques (Sorbonne), September 1994, unpub.

Thiriez, Régine. "The Qianlong Emperor's European Palaces." In *The Delights of Harmony: The European Palaces of the Yuanmingyuan and the Jesuits at the 18th Century Court of Beijing*. Worcester Mass: College of the Holy Cross, 1994: 6–17.

Thiriez, Régine, and Durand, Antoine. "Engraving the Emperor of China's European Palaces." *Biblion, The New York Public Library Bulletin*, 1, no. 2 (Spring 1993): 81–107.

Thiriez, Régine. "The German Ambassador's Vision of China: Mumm von Schwarzenstein's Photographic Album, 1900–1902." *Visual Resources*, 9 (1993): 273–289.

Thiriez, Régine. *Les photographes occidentaux des Palais européens du Yuanmingyuan, catalogue raisonné des photographies, 1860–1911*. DEA at EPHE, Sorbonne, May 1991, unpub.

Thiriez, Régine. "Les palais européens du Yuanmingyuan à travers la photographie: 1860–1940." *Arts Asiatiques*, 45 (1990): 90–96.

Thiriez, Régine. "Ernst Ohlmer, ein Amateur-Fotograph im Alten Pekin." *Hildesheimer 1991 Heimat-kalender*, 1990: 87–92.

Thomson, John. *Foochow and the River Min*. London: Autotype Fine Art Co., 1873.

Thomson, John. *Illustrations of China and its People. A Series of Photographs with Letterpress Descriptive of the Places and People Represented*. London, 1874.

Thomson, John. *Through China with a Camera*. Westminter: Constable, 1898.

Thomson, John. *China and its People*. London: British Council, 1991.

Thomson, John, and Smith, Adolphe. *Street Life in London*. London: Sampson Low, 1878.

Tsao Muh Tuh. *The Old Summer Palace*. Peking: Tsing Hua College, 1915 unpub. ms.

Uitzinger, Ellen. "For the Man who has Everything: Western-style Exotica in Birthday Celebrations at the Court of Ch'ien-lung." In Blussé, Leonard and Zurndorfer, Harriet T. *Conflict and Accomodation in Early Modern East Asia*. Leiden, New York, Köln: E.J. Brill, 1993: 216–239.

Van Monckoven, D. *Traité général de photographie*. Paris: V. Masson & fils, 1873.

Les vues stéréoscopiques de Ferrier et Soulier, catalogue 1851–1870. Paris: Editions du Palmier en Zinc, 1992.

Varin, Paul [Du Pin, Colonel]. *Expédition de Chine*. Paris: Michel Lévy Frères, 1862.

Vetch, Col. R.H. *Life, letters and diaries of Lieutenant General Sir Gerald Graham*. Edinburgh & London: Wm. Blackwood & Sons, 1901.

Wang, Tao. *Yingruan zazhi* (Shanghai Miscellany). Shanghai, 1862 (repr. Shanghai, 1989).

White, Stephen. "The Far East, A Magazine of the Orient for European Eyes." *Images*, 1991: 1–2, 39–47.

White, Stephen. "Felix Beato and the First Korean War, 1871." *The Photographic Collector*, 1982: 1, 76–85.

Wiesner, Ulrich. *Chinesisches Porzellan; die Olmer'sche Sammlung im Roemer-Museum, Hildesheim*. Mainz am Rhein, Philip von Zabern, 1981.

[Wilkinson, William Henry]. *"Where Chineses Drive." English Student-life in Pekin, by a Student-interpreter*. London: W.H. Allen, 1885.

Williams, C.A.S. *Chinese Tribute*. London: Literary Services and Productions, 1969.

Williamson A. *Journeys in North China*. 2 vol. London, 1870.

Wolseley, Garnet J. *Narrative of the War with China in 1860*. London: Longman & Roberts, 1862.

Worswick, Clark, and Spence, Jonathan. *Imperial China: Photographs 1850–1912*. New York: Pennwick Publishing, 1978.

Wright, Stanley F. *Hart and the Chinese Customs*. Belfast: Mullan & Son, 1950.

Zannier, Italo. *Le Grand Tour*. Venezia: Canal & Stamperia Editrice, Paris: Canal Editions, Paris 1997.

Index

C

S

T

U

V

W

X

Y

Z